Newbury House series on

ONVERBAL BEHAVIOR

The aim of this new series, under the general editorship of Thomas A. Sebeok, of Indiana University, is to publish original monographs and collections dealing with nonverbal messages by means of which all living beings interact.

The first book compares social behavior in Brazil and the United States. Subsequent works will include a handbook on nonverbal communication directed toward teachers of foreign languages, the purpose of which is to introduce techniques for imparting to students of foreign languages the importance of appropriate nonverbal responses for successful communication between cultures.

The third volume, a handbook on Japanese nonverbal communication, will apply these techniques to daily conduct in Japan. Included are such topics as posture and bowing, behavior in a private home or public place, eye contact, and a selection of Japanese emblematic gestures. The fourth volume will examine the culture of the area surrounding the Gulf of Arabia from the same viewpoint.

Future directions the series will take include an extension of nonverbal analyses to other foreign speech communities, notably China, and to areas of culture contact between different groups within the United States. A long-range goal is to encourage the publication of basic studies on nonverbal communication by the foremost authorities now writing in this extremely active field.

D0711171

BEHAVING BRAZILIAN

A COMPARISON OF BRAZILIAN AND NORTH AMERICAN SOCIAL BEHAVIOR

Phyllis A. Harrison

Richard Vidutis
Illustrator/Researcher

NEWBURY HOUSE PUBLISHERS
A division of HarperCollins*Publishers*

Library of Congress Cataloging in Publication Data

Harrison-Brose, Phyllis A., 1951-
  Behaving Brazilian

  (Nonverbal behavior)
  Includes bibliographical references.
  1. National characteristics, Brazilian. 2. National
characteristics, American. 3. Nonverbal communication--
Brazil. 4. Nonverbal communication--United States.
5. Interviews--Brazil.. I. Title. II. Series.
F2510.H37 1983   303.4'8281'073   83-13301
ISBN 0-88377-315-5

Cover and interior book design by Kenneth Wilson

NEWBURY HOUSE PUBLISHERS
A division of HarperCollins*Publishers*

Language Science
Language Teaching
Language Learning

Printed in the U.S.A.
63-22655

First printing: November 1983
6 7 8 9 10 11 12 13 14 15 16

Grateful acknowledgement is due to the following individuals who contributed their time and expertise in the evaluation of our manuscript. Their comments, suggestions, and corrections have greatly improved the accuracy and readability of this text.

Leopoldo M. Bernucci, University of Michigan
Nelson Cerqueira, Indiana University
Antônio Amaro Cirugião, University of Connecticut
Fred M. Clark, University of North Carolina
Alfred Hower, University of Florida
Kenneth David Jackson, University of Texas
John B. Jensen, Florida International University
Randal Johnson, Rutgers
Dale A. Koike, University of California/Santa Barbara
John W. Martin, University of Arizona
Emilio Moran, Indiana University
Vivian Payne, Cummins Engines Company, Columbus, Indiana
Richard A. Preto-Rodas, University of South Florida
Monica Rector, Pontifícia Universidade Católica do Rio de Janeiro
Karl J. Reinhardt, University of Houston
Candace Slater, University of Pennsylvania
Jon Tolman, University of New Mexico
Aluízio Ramos Trinta, Universidade Federal do Rio de Janeiro
Luiz F. Valente, Providence College

CONTENTS

INTRODUCTION

It is a very true and expressive phrase, "He looked daggers at me," for the first pattern and prototype of all daggers must have been a glance of the eye. First, there was the glance of Jove's eye, then his fiery bolt, then, the material gradually hardening, tridents, spears, javelins, and finally, for the convenience of private men, daggers, krisses, and so forth, were invented. It is wonderful how we get about the streets without being wounded by these delicate and glancing weapons, a man can so nimbly whip out his rapier, or without being noticed carry it unsheathed. Yet it is rare that one gets seriously looked at.

Henry David Thoreau
A Week on the Concord and Merrimac Rivers

Rarely do we examine one another carefully, consciously recording each bit of information the eye receives or each bit that we transmit to others through our gestures, expressions, postures, and the like. Yet much of the information that we receive and transmit travels through a visual rather than an oral or aural medium. Nonverbal communication is performed and seen rather than spoken and heard, and studies have suggested that such information accounts for as much as sixty-five percent of interpersonal communication.[1] Students and teachers of Brazilian Portuguese, as well as other North Americans like tourists and business people who interact with Brazilians, will profit from a careful reading of this handbook. The following pages describe gestures, behaviors, and situations vital to Brazilian-North American communication but often passed over in language and culture classes.

The following examples show the importance of nonverbal communication between members of the two cultures: An American exchange student in Brazil sits in a high school geography class, waiting nervously for the teacher to hand out an exam. She has studied diligently for the test, with much help from a Brazilian friend who is also in the class. As she reads the exam, a look of relief spreads across her face. She looks over at her friend, smiles, and gives an American gesture meaning "O.K.!"—a circle made with thumb and index finger. The Brazilian blushes, stares, and drops her gaze. To her, the gesture is an obscene one, meaning roughly, "Screw you!"

A Brazilian sees an American friend on the far side of a crowded room. The Brazilian raises one outstretched hand and waves with a scooping motion. The American cheerfully waves a response. The Brazilian continues to wave. The American smiles and waves again. The Brazilian continues to wave. The American smiles but begins to feel rather silly. Finally, the Brazilian strides impatiently across the room saying, "I want to talk to you!" The Brazilian gesture means specifically that.

Different cultures also organize, mark, and perceive time in different ways, reflecting different value systems.

An American, hurrying to keep a lunch appointment, sees a Brazilian friend in a hallway. The American flashes a quick smile, says, "Hello, how are you, I must run, I have a lunch appointment," and rushes off, perhaps leaving the Brazilian friend feeling somewhat offended or taken aback. While the American considers the appointment a valid reason for delaying a visit, the Brazilian considers a visit with a friend far more important than the punctual keeping of an appointment. If questioned, the American would probably say, "Oh, those Brazilians. They are always late. They don't care about being on time or keeping others waiting." If the Brazilian were asked to comment, he would likely say, "Oh, those Americans. They are so cold. They care more about business than about friends."

The following observations from Edward T. Hall show that such contrasting attitudes extend beyond personal encounters to whole systems of thought and behavior. American business practices can interfere with business in Brazil.

For example, American Foreign Service officers assigned to Latin America should be out interacting with the local people, but because of immutable bureaucratic custom they can't leave their desks. Cut off from the people with whom they are supposed to be establishing ties, how can they be effective?[2]

They cannot be effective in Brazil, where personal ties are a necessary prelude to business.

The built environment can also contain nonverbal messages, and these too are subject to misinterpretation.

> The Latin house is often built around a patio that is next to the sidewalk but hidden from outsiders behind a wall . . . American Point Four Technicians living in Latin America used to complain that they felt "left out" of things, that they were "shut out."[3]

They were indeed shut out, but the walls were not statements against Americans or strangers as much as they were statements *for* the great respect and privacy accorded to family in Brazil. No Brazilian would ever expect the casual admittance to family circles and to the family home that is common in the United States.

Brazil is, of course, a Western country colonized by Europeans, the Portuguese. Thus, the many cultural differences between Brazil and the United States are not always as dramatic as the differences between the United States and an Eastern country like Japan, where a smile can indicate embarrassment or confusion; or a Middle Eastern country, like Saudi Arabia, where the left hand is rarely used except for personal hygiene; or an indigenous American civilization, like the Navaho, among whom competition is avoided and any drawing of attention to oneself (as students volunteering an answer in class) is cause for discomfort. Still, many differences do exist between the United States and Brazil, and if they are more subtle, they are also less expected and can easily lead to miscommunication, frustration, and sometimes ill will.

Despite the importance of nonverbal elements in communication, they rarely receive much attention in language classes. If they are discussed, they are often couched as a footnote or an aside, or a particular gesture or greeting is taught without reference to the whole nonverbal system of which it is a part. Students learn grammar, vocabulary, and syntax; they practice speaking, hearing, and writing; less often do they learn gestures, or practice gesturing; rarely, if ever, do they practice looking, standing, or touching by different cultural rules. Thomas A. Sebeok has described this imbalance:

> The question, then boils down to this: if, as is the case, we lavish incalculable amounts of energy, time, and money

to instill in children and adults a range of foreign language competencies, why are the indissolubly parallel foreign gesticulatory skills all but universally neglected, especially considering that even linguists are fully aware that what has been called the total communication package, "best likened to a coaxial cable carrying many messages at the same time" is hardly an exaggerated simile?[4]

Individuals wishing to familiarize themselves with Brazilian-Portuguese nonverbal communication will find few English language materials to draw upon. Sandra T. Bunker's gestural inventory contains some good suggestions for the teaching of gestures, as well as some gestures common both to Brazil and other parts of Latin America, but her emphasis is on Spanish-speaking countries rather than Portuguese-speaking Brazil.[5] A brief article by Percilia Santos on figurative language and gestures describes fifteen gestures and the phrases that often accompany them, but the article does not purport to be exhaustive and gives only a brief description of the Brazilian worldview of which the gestures are typical.[6] Edward Hall's studies of proxemics often describe Latin American examples that hold true for Brazil. *The Silent Language* and *Beyond Culture* are particularly helpful in detailing the Latin American worldview, but his concern lies with drawing the larger picture, so the myriad details of daily interaction are not described in his work. A study of time and punctuality by Robert V. Levine, Laurin J. West, and Harry T. Reis gives an interesting account of several experiments measuring the constrasting attitudes found in the two cultures.[7]

A more general study of national characteristics by José Honório Rodrigues, *The Brazilians: Their Character and Aspirations*, does not look specifically at nonverbal communication but does give a detailed explanation of the Brazilian worldview past and present that sheds light on many aspects of Brazilian nonverbal communication.[8] A good general study of Brazil is Charles Wagley's *An Introduction to Brazil*.[9] Selden Rodman, in *The Brazil Traveler: History, Culture, Literature and the Arts*, provides a brief but informative overview of Brazil's development.[10] Two more detailed studies, each including extensive bibliographies, are Rollie E. Poppino, *Brazil: The Land and the People* and Caio Prado Jr., *The Colonial Background of Modern Brazil*.[11] Gilberto Freyre's studies of Brazilian cultural development (cf.

The Masters and the Slaves, New World in the Tropics, and particularly *The Mansions and the Shanties)* will help the American to understand Brazilian behavior through an understanding of Brazilian culture.[12]

The lack of material devoted to the studying, recording, and teaching of Brazilian nonverbal communication means that North Americans may find themselves unable to communicate effectively in Brazil even if they achieve verbal fluency in Brazilian Portuguese. Lacking nonverbal expertise, Americans will find themselves at a cultural impasse when they stand too far away, shake hands infrequently and not warmly enough, fill a day with appointments and try to get each thing done quickly in order to get on to the next. American men often jump back from a Brazilian man's *abraço*, and American women sometimes jump back from the kiss of greeting tendered by Brazilian women.

This handbook attempts to remedy this lack of nonverbal expertise by bringing together a body of material on Brazilian nonverbal communication and social behavior gathered from interviews with Brazilians and with North Americans who have spent time in Brazil. The interview method, while enabling us to compile a quantity of data, did present some limitations. Often the behavior described is formal or "polite," not necessarily what one will find among family members watching television on a typical evening. Most of us, after all, tend to present a positive cultural picture when describing our country to foreigners. At times we received conflicting information. The gesture known in Brazil as "the banana" and elsewhere as "the forearm jerk" or "the royal shaft" is a good example. We have indicated such conflicting data, though we could not always explain or resolve the conflict. Other points raised during interviews concerned matters of behavior that are learned at a very early age and so taken for granted as "normal" behavior and performed almost unconsciously. *Specific* information in such areas as eye contact, touching, and personal distance is not readily accessible through the interview method, and our experiments with videotape proved less successful than we had hoped in eliciting pertinent data. Although we notice immediately when our own rules are violated, we may be unable to specify the precise distance and/or duration that changes a glance to a stare or a comfortable conversational distance to one of intimacy or of "breathing down my neck." As a result, our presentation of such data is in relative terms like "closer" and "longer."

As the above remarks indicate, our use of "nonverbal communication" includes gesture, body posture, body contact, and proxemics. We have also included subjects like dress, audience behavior, and table settings which, though they do not precisely fit the currently popular concept of nonverbal communication as body language, still constitute significant ways of communicating outside the verbal channel. We have excluded those nonverbal elements that are beyond conscious control and imitation (i.e., physiological or chemical responses such as pupil dilation or sweat). Because we could not hope to cover the entire range of Brazilian behavior, or even the entire range of Brazilian gestures, we have concentrated our inquiries on areas of contrast between the two cultures, those being the areas most likely to cause the foreigner problems. In addition, we have included background material on Brazil and Brazilians so that the reader can begin to grasp the verbal and nonverbal systems as two aspects of a larger whole.

The reader must be aware that behavior changes over time. We have tried to avoid including material that resulted from a passing trend, and when such material is included, we have pointed out its possibly temporary status. Chances are, however, that some small portions of this material may be outdated by the time this manuscript goes to press or the reader of it to Brazil. The reader must also be aware that Brazil is larger than the continental United States and just as varied, containing many regions, ethnic groups, and socio-economic classes. Describing a typical Brazilian is like describing a typical American—"typical" depends on region, income, race, religion, and individual preference. No analysis made by a foreign observer could hope to cover all the variations in behavior found in these different groups, and even if such coverage were possible, the resulting study would be far too lengthy and complex to serve as an introductory handbook.

The Brazilians we interviewed were primarily from the upper and upper-middle socioeconomic classes, and most were from the Rio/São Paulo area. They are representative of many Brazilians and of the regions and classes that most North Americans will encounter in Brazil, but that is not to say that they are representative of all Brazilians. Some segments of the Brazilian population, particularly the lower socio-economic classes, and some aspects of Brazilian society, like the problem of poverty, receive little attention in this volume. The reader should be cautioned against assuming that the materials contained in this study represent immutable facts about all Brazil and all Brazilians. Many of the persons interviewed wished to remain anonymous, so we have indicated quotations from interviews but have given only the most limited description of the interviewee quoted.

In organizing our material, we have tried to design chapters as self-contained units, so the reader interested in business practices can go first to the chapter on business. As a result, the reader who begins with the Overview and proceeds through the text will find some repetitions of general, explanatory material and of specific points that are relevant to several areas. We feel that repetition in a work such as this is far preferable to omission.

Thanks are due to the United States Department of Education that provided funding for our research. The research reported herein was performed pursuant to a grant from the U.S. Department of Education as a part of the International Research and Studies Program under the authority of Title VI, Section 605, of the Higher Education Act of 1965. Thanks are also due to Dr. Emilio Moran who offered advice and encouragement through the project, to Augusta Ribeiro de Jesus, who helped with interviews, suggestions, typing, and the editing of the Portuguese, to Dr. Sahnny Johnson who gave us the benefit of her previous experience with nonverbal communication research, and most of all to the Americans and Brazilians who answered and reanswered our endless questions about Brazil.

Erving Goffman has observed that "Life may not be much of a gamble, but interaction is."[13] This handbook will certainly not remove the gamble from interaction, but it should at least help to even up the odds.

NOTES

1. Albert Mehrabian, "Commuication without Words," *Psychology Today* 2 (1968), 52–55; appears in Sahnny Johnson, *Nonverbal Communication in the Teaching of English as a Foreign Language* (forthcoming).

2. Edward T. Hall, *Beyond Culture* (Garden City, N.Y.: Anchor Press/Doubleday and Co., Inc., 1976), p. 19.

3. _____, *The Silent Language* (Garden City, N.Y.: Doubleday and Co., Inc., 1959), p. 199.

4. Thomas A. Sebeok, "The Semiotic Web," *Contributions to the Doctrine of Signs* (Lisse: Peter de Ridder Press, 1976), p. 179.

5. Sandra T. Bunker, *An Illustrated Gestural Inventory: Latin American Gestures for English Speaking Students of Spanish* (M.A. Thesis, Brigham Young University, 1978).

6. Percilia Santos, "Examples of Figurative Language and Gestures which Characterize the Brazilian People," *American Foreign Language Teacher* 4 (1973), 22–25.

7. Robert V. Levine, Laurin J. West, and Harry T. Reis, "Perceptions of Time and Punctuality in the United States and Brazil," *Journal of Personality and Social Psychology* 38 (1980), 541–50.

8. José Honório Rodrigues, *The Brazilians: Their Character and Aspirations*, trans. Ralph Edward Dimmick (Austin: Univ. of Texas Press, 1967).

9. Charles Wagley, *An Introduction to Brazil* (New York: Columbia Univ. Press, 1963; rev. ed. 1971).

10. Selden Rodman, *The Brazil Traveler: History, Culture, Literature, and the Arts* (Old Greenwich, CT: The Devin-Adair Co., 1975).

11. Rollie E. Poppino, *Brazil: The Land and the People* (New York: University Press, 1968), Caio Prado Jr., *The Colonial Background of Modern Brazil* (Berkeley and Los Angeles: University of California Press, 1967).

12. Gilberto Freyre, *Brazil: An Interpretation* (New York: Alfred A. Knopf, 1945), *The Mansions and the Shanties: The Making of Modern Brazil*, Harriet do Onis trans. (New York: Alfred A. Knopf, 1963), *The Masters and the Slaves: A Study in the Development of Brazilian Civilization*, Samual Putnam, trans. (New York: Alfred A. Knopf, 1956, 1963), *New World in the Tropics: The Culture of Modern Brazil* (New York: Alfred A. Knopf, 1966).

13. Erving Goffman, *The Presentation of Self in Everyday Life* (Garden City, New York: Doubleday and Co., Inc., 1969), p. 241.

BEHAVING BRAZILIAN

OVERVIEW

Regions in Brazil

Brazil, larger than the continental United States, combines geographic, climatic, economic, and ethnic variations that give Brazilians and those who study Brazil a strong sense of regions. Regions defined by geography, climate, economics, and ethnic variation are discussed by writers like Charles Wagley, Sheldon Rodman, and Rollie Poppino. Because our study concerns the ways Brazilians interact, our concern has been with regions perceived by Brazilians—Brazilian stereotypes, if you will, of Brazil.

One major division splits north and south, though the precise division depends upon whether you ask a Brazilian from São Paulo, Belo Horizonte, or Brasília, for some draw a line just above Rio, describing everything beyond it as the North, some draw the line at Belo Horizonte, and still others draw the line at Brasília. One man from Sao Paulo described Brazil as "two Brazils—the São Paulo/Rio area and the rest."

Another major division distinguishes coastal Brazil from interior Brazil, and this division applies in both North and South. The majority of the population lives along the coast, so urban and developed areas tend to be on or near the coast though some notable examples, like Brasília and Manaus, do exist. A few hours traveling inland from Sao Paulo leads to a very different portion of Brazil, characterized by small towns and rural areas where living patterns differ markedly from living patterns in the cities, and differ much more than in the United States where "small towns have everything you need." According to one Brazilian, "the interior is another Brazil. People are friendlier, more open, more hospitable...They expect you to visit, to eat, to stay." Because the distinction is actually one of rural/urban rather than interior/-coastal, the capitals of interior states tend to be more like coastal urban areas than like the rest of the interior.

North/South regional patterns in Brazil are just the reverse of North/South patterns in the United States. Southerners view the North as less developed, with smaller towns, large rural areas, little economic development or opportunity, and a resulting lack of emphasis on education. While the foregoing description is accurate for much of the North, a distinction must be made between the stereotype and the reality. Northern Brazil does contain large urban areas like Belem, Manaus, Fortaleza, Recife, Maranhão and Salvador, while the South contains large rural areas which, as mentioned above, differ greatly from the urban centers. Brazilians in general place a high value on education, and if the North lacks educational facilities, the lack is because of economic factors rather than choice. Within the North, ethnic variation marks a number of divisions. A widely-held belief about the far North is that it is largely populated by descendents of Portuguese colonists and early settlers. Brazil's purest Portuguese, according to some Brazilians, is spoken in the North, especially in Maranhão. The Northeast, particularly Bahia, is characterized by a strong Black influence, stemming from the importation of African slaves in the eighteenth century. Northerners are sometimes teased about their region by other Brazilians, who equate rural with backward and less competitive with lazy.

The South is described as urban and industrial. The largest urban centers, São Paulo and Rio, are in the South, and these cities are considered to be the cultural, intellectual, and economic centers of Brazil. The South has received the greatest influence in recent times from foreign cultures, both from waves of immigrants from Europe and from the Orient, and from international business and economic concerns.

Within the South, a friendly and traditional rivalry exists between Sao Paulo and Rio. People from São Paulo, described as busy, hardworking, and efficient, are called *paulistas* or *paulistanos*. Technically, *paulistas* are people from the State of São Paulo while *paulistanos* are people from the city, but many Brazilians ignore this distinction. "In São Paulo, they run, not walk." "In São Paulo, everyone is busy working and making money." São Paulo is the center of industry in Brazil, and just as in many parts of the United States, industrialization has subordinated many individual preferences and cultural traits to suit the needs of the larger system. São Paulo is probably more like the

United States than are other parts of Brazil, though the differences are still greater than the similarities. Before the building of Brasília, Rio was the capital of Brazil. When the capital moved, Rio changed from a governmental center to a tourist center, a resort city; at the same time, it is an increasingly important industrial city. People from Rio, called *cariocas*, are described as relaxed, carefree, and friendly. "People worry less and enjoy themselves more." Some Brazilians say that *paulistas* work hard to make money and then go to Rio to spend it. A *paulista* described the two types as follows. "*Cariocas* are so-so. It depends on the person. Many *paulistas* think they are lazy. *Cariocas* think *paulistas* are industrious, hard working." A *carioca* provided the following comment. "*Paulistas* are very conservative. *Paulistas* like *cariocas*, especially *paulista* men like *carioca* women."

One should consider these Brazilian stereotypes in the same light as one considers American stereotypes regarding New Yorkers, Californians, Texans, Yankees, and the like. They are generalizations, referred to more often in jest than in serious conversation. Still, they are based upon certain very broad regional characteristics.

Social Organization

The concepts of class and status are strong in Brazil, influencing many other aspects of Brazilian life. Jobs are accorded a particular status, and an upper or middle class person would not perform a lower class job. For instance, one Brazilian horrified her parents by taking a part-time job in the United States doing janitorial work while going to school. Another Brazilian student in the United States was delivering newspapers for extra money, something he would not consider doing in Brazil. Upper class children and young adults generally do not work, partly because they are expected to put their efforts into their studies, and partly because of the jobs that would be available to them. Jobs such as babysitting or waiting tables, so often filled by students in the United States, are considered lower class jobs in Brazil, the status being determined by the wages (Brazil has a much lower minimum wage, and a worker may earn more than one minimum wage for a particular job) and the manual labor involved. Upper and upper-middle class women who go to work after or instead of college would probably not take a secretarial position, as such a position lacks status. Differences in language, dress, and behavior are often attributed to class.

Classes within Brazilian society are described first in economic terms, although family name is important in some circles, particularly amongst those who are descendants of the early Portuguese colonists and settlers. For the majority of Brazilians, however, class and income are mutually determinate, though what constitutes a specific class will, of course, vary from region to region. What is high class in Vitória might be middle class in São Paulo.

Interaction between classes is not great, except within specific roles such as employee/maid, customer/sales clerk, or customer/waiter. One Brazilian suggested this lack of interaction might account for the lack of informal exchanges like "Have a nice day!" that one hears so often in the United States and so often between relative strangers. One phrase that is heard frequently in cross-class situations is *Você sabe com quem está falando?* (Do you know who you're talking to?), used when the speaker senses a lack of respect. A lower status person (whatever his specific status) may use *doutor* (doctor) when addressing a person of higher status. The title shows social deference and may have nothing to do with educational degrees or specific professions. Most North Americans in Brazil will interact closely only with members of the upper and upper-middle classes, except in those situations noted above, when the general attitudes are formal, distant, and sometimes paternal.

Brazilians see racial prejudice in the United States that they do not see in Brazil. "In Brazil, Blacks and Whites are open and friendly. When you approach [a North American Black], they move away. Once they know you're a foreigner, they become more open." Black and White Brazilians sense a strained relationship between Blacks and Whites in the United States that they do not sense in Brazil. Charles Wagley observes that although only four official categories are used to describe Brazil's racial mixture, unofficial usage may employ far more to distinguish racial mixtures and shades of difference between them. Attitudes and terms vary from region to region, but throughout Brazil

> Color is but one of the criteria by which people are placed in the total social hierarchy.... A Brazilian is never merely a white man or a man of color; he is a rich, well-educated white man from the *povo*; he is a well-educated

mulatto with a good job, or a poor, uneducated Negro. Other criteria, such as income, education, family connections, and even personal charm and special abilities or aptitudes come into play when placing a person in terms of the prestige hierarchy or even of social class. Above all, these multiple criteria determine who will be admitted to hotels, restaurants, and most social clubs; who will get preferential treatment in stores, churches, nightclubs, and travel conveyances; and who will have the best chance among a number of marriage suitors. . . . In effect, there are no Brazilian social groups based on skin color alone, although, to the casual visitor, this would not seem to be true.[1]

Brazil has changed considerably since the time of Wagley's observations, and Florestan Fernandes, in a 1979 follow-up to his 1951 study of Black/White relations in Brazil, finds improvements, but also finds discrimination a real factor in Brazilian life. He writes that "Racial stereotypes have not totally disappeared and they still produce devastating effects on the aspirations of the Negro. But they no longer automatically serve to exclude him from certain positions in the labor force."[2] In comparison with other racial groups in Brazil, Fernandes observes that "The stereotypes and stigmas have lessened as these groups have increased in size. But, in the case of Negro, this kind of acceptance is not yet a reality."[3]

José Honório Rodrigues, whose book provides an overview of Brazilian society, summarizes the situation thus: "The limited degree of racial intolerance or color discrimination that exists has economic and social bases; those who overcome disadvantage by education find the gates of society open to them."[4]

Because the class structure is so strong in Brazil, one Brazilian with extensive travel experience both within and outside Brazil suggested that Americans in Brazil be particularly conscious of dressing in accord with Brazilian style and fashion, perhaps even overdressing by casual American standards, lest assumptions be made regarding their economic status and/or class.

Machismo

Although male and female roles are changing in Brazil, they are still well defined and strongly traditional when compared to their North American counterparts, and North American women and men are bound to experience some difficulty adjusting to Brazilian patterns. Brazilians themselves are aware of varying degrees to which a man lives the traditional *macho* role, and while one young Brazilian man observed that "a look from a man is enough to make a woman keep still," others thought his statement a bit extreme. Further, one North American anthropologist who has spent much time in Brazil remarked that from his observations, Brazilian women often took a dominant role, particularly in family matters, and that Brazilian women often have things their way. Brazilian women suggest that when a women knows how to handle a *macho* man, she can control the situation though she seems to be under his control. North Americans in Brazil must be aware that most Brazilians are knowledgeable of North American roles and patterns, but are not necessarily impressed by them. Young Brazilians tend to be less inclined to adopt the traditional roles, but these roles still pervade Brazilian society, in obvious and subtle ways.

The Brazilian man demonstrates his strength through aggressive pursuit and courteous respect. He must be the aggressor in all senses (or, as some women say, must think he is the aggressor), so he must be the one to take the initiative in a business deal, in problem solving, in courtship. Brazilian men watching North American movies (shown widely in Brazil) may protest loudly if the heroine takes the obvious initiative. A Brazilian woman initiates flirtations through subtle but effective means like eye contact. Men are expected to make passes at women, and a man may very well make a pass at a woman he has no interest in and whom he expects will refuse him. Men— particularly young men or men from lower socio-economic classes—may stare at, whistle at, and comment upon women they see in public. At the same time, the man's superior strength means he must show courtesy to women, particularly to women of an equal class or status. Men open doors, help with coats, carry packages, and always pay the bills. Such actions demonstrate strength and respect for women. They are viewed as social courtesies in Brazil and most Brazilian women expect them. One woman commented that "it makes the man feel important, and the woman feel like a woman." While several Brazilians told these North American interviewers that they found the North American system more relaxed and more comfortable, several also commented that "men here don't show any courtesy to women" and that Brazilian women in the United States feel that "men here don't notice women at all." The *macho* man shows his strength by the way he interacts with women. At the same time, he is much freer than the North American man to express his emotions—to laugh, to cry, to hug a friend—and less concerned with maintaining a calm, controlled exterior.

The Brazilian woman displays her femininity through feminine beauty and grace, accentuated by tighter fitting and more revealing clothes than the North American is used to seeing or wearing, frequent and lavish use of cosmetics and jewelry, and a concern for a graceful appearance when sitting, standing, or walking. These concerns stem in part from an awareness of being watched closely and constantly by men and other women. While a woman is expected to display her charms, she must not take any direct or obvious initiative in approaching a man. Doing so risks being labelled "fast" or "loose," as the second component in traditional Brazilian femininity is dependence on the man. Displays of physical strength detract from a woman's femininity, so Brazilian women expect the courtesies like door-opening. Brazilians are not impressed by the increasingly frequent North American attitude that such courtesies are demeaning and see that attitude as pushy, unfeeling, and unfeminine. Brazilian men are offended by a refusal of such courtesies, particularly if a woman insists upon paying a bill. Brazilian women often do not plan careers (at least, not long-term careers) in the business world, as the majority will marry, after which their primary responsibilities will be home and family. Brazilian women are not involved in sports to the same degree that North American women are. Some swim, though not competitively, and some do participate in organized gymanastics and volleyball competitions. Girls and women are not encouraged to participate in more strenuous sports like basketball or soccer. One Brazilian man remembered seeing a women's soccer team once or twice, but that was a specific publicity play. "A women's soccer team would be a joke in Brazil." North American women who plan to spend much time in Brazil, especially women who will be working in Brazil, must learn to work within the Brazilian system, where femininity often means fragility or a fragile front.

Within this system, perhaps because of the expectations of teasing and flirtatious behavior, jealousy can be a problem. The line between complimentary flirting, expected by women of men, and overly aggressive or overly direct behavior, grounds for a jealous reaction especially from husband or boyfriend, is often a fine one. Men and women often form separate groups at a party, as do married couples and dating couples. The explanation for the separation is that "they have nothing in common," but it helps to ease possible jealous tensions. A North American woman who accompanies her businessman husband to Brazil must be aware of this potential problem and should never flirt with her husband's business associates. Both men and women might very well construe such behavior as promiscuous.

Because they often overstep the line, North American men are accused by Brazilian women of expecting immediate sexual involvements, "even on the first date." While interaction between Brazilian men and women is much more suggestive than between North Americans, North Americans actually have a more casual attitude about sexual encounters. Brazilians are very couple oriented, but do not make the equation between romance and sex that North Americans almost automatically do. Sexual mores are changing in Brazil, and unmarried couples living together are becoming more common. Still, the phenomenon is not as common (or at least not as public) there as here, and many Brazilian men adopt the attitude that a man must protect the woman he wants to marry, that he can go to a prostitute if he so desires. North American women do have a reputation in Brazil for being free and perhaps even promiscuous (though North American men are stereotyped as naive), a reputation that stems from American films shown in Brazil and also from the behavior of Americans in Brazil. While some groups in Brazilian society accept a relatively casual attitude toward premarital relations, a North American woman should realize that such a situation is potentially far more damaging in Brazil than in the United States.

Romantic relationships tend to be more possessive in Brazil than in North America. Couples go everywhere together and do everything together, and for a woman, this often means that her boyfriend's circle of friends becomes her circle of friends. Couples keep in daily contact through visits, dates, and telephone calls. Women rarely go out alone, so the woman without a boyfriend may find her social life rather curtailed. "Your whole life revolves around that relationship. When it ends, you have nothing." Romantic attachments often form between members of the extended family, such as second, third and fourth cousins, and more distant cousins often marry. Such attachments strengthen the family unit and the marriage bond by making the family sphere the social sphere as well.

American women must accept the fact that they will be propositioned by both single and married men. What Americans refer to as "the double standard" is strong in Brazil: men are expected to "play the field" both before and after marriage, but for a married woman to have an affair is unacceptable. "Her husband would give her back to her parents." "She'd be divorced for sure." Her affair reflects badly on her husband as well. "If he took care of her, she wouldn't fool around." Divorce, legalized in 1977, is more expensive, more complicated, and is not accepted as easily as it is in North America. Family networks are far too strong in Brazil to permit the easy dissolution of marriage bonds.

Family and Friends

The Brazilian family network is much larger and much closer than in North America. "Family" means parents, children, grand-parents, aunts, uncles, cousins, second, third, and fourth cousins, plus spouses and siblings of all of these. Charles Wagley notes that Brazilians "have sometimes used the term *parentela* (kinship group) or even 'clan' to describe these larger groups."[5] Several generations may live under one roof, and when family members leave the home, they try to settle within close proximity. Children and young adults remain at home until marriage, and after marriage make frequent visits home—at least one a week if possible. Perhaps because the network is so large, one finds little rivalry and many close relationships in a Brazilian family. Most Brazilians feel a strong sense of family loyalty and consider it an automatic duty to help family members in any way possible. One's closest personal friends are likely to come from this extended family network. "Outsiders without kinship connec-tions may find that Latin American cities and towns have a restricted social life. Once one has been received into a family through an intimate friend, however, social life may become quite intense."[6] The family network may be further extended through a system of godparents, *compadres* and *comadres*, which entails much closer involvements than does the North American system of godparents.

"Friend" likewise means something very different to a Brazilian. "A friend is like a brother or sister. You can share things, be honest with them. They will accept you as you are. They will question you, argue with you. It leads to growth." "We are much closer to our friends than you are." North Americans unaccustomed to the Brazilian styles of greeting, to their general warmth and enthusiasm, and to the Brazilian notion of what constitutes a good friend often assume that Brazilians feel close friendship with nearly everyone, but this is not precisely the case. Brazilians do form friendly relationships easily, but they also distinguish levels of friendship, as North Americans distinguish between an acquaintance and a friend. The parallel, however, is not exact. *Colega* translates as fellow or colleague, a "little friend," as one Brazilian phrased it. One has many *colegas* through school or job, or through the trading of favors. Networks of family and friends are also important; one gains *colegas* through *colegas*. *Colegas* may give you advice and ask about you—what you are doing, where you are going—and you may have coffee or dinner with them, but that does not indicate close friendship, and friendship certainly does not come automatically with a job or with school, as is often the case in the United States. *Colega* names a much closer relationship than what the North American intends by "acquaintance," perhaps nearer to what the North American intends by "friend," since *colegas* do share obligations and responsibilities. A woman from Belo Horizonte told of asking neighbors to lend her an alarm clock, as she needed to be up at six the following morning. None had a clock to lend her, but at five the next morning, people began knocking on her door to see that she was awake and at seven were still checking to be sure she had awakened on time. Brazilians do not understand the American concept of casual friendship or acquaintanceship without mutual obligations.

In Brazil, a real friend, an *amigo(a)*, is "somebody you can really count on who is with you always." While all friends are called *amigos*, all Brazilians know the distinction between an *amigo(a)* and a *colega*. An *amigo(a)* is "like family" and may well be family—a second cousin or a family member through the system of godparents. One American in Brazil noticed a big difference between "school" friends and "family" friends. The former she would visit at school, and they might go shopping after school, but they would not visit one another's homes. "School friends were not the same as family or neighborhood friends," and family friends —friends within the family—"were the most important of all." A person has only one or two true *amigos*, for a true friend is "someone you have taken time to build a special, solid relationship with, not superficial. Not someone you've known a year or two. Someone you've grown up with." It is often a life-long relationship and creates a degree of mutual involvement that few North Americans find outside the immediate family. Friends are absolutely at home in one another's houses, and friends know all about one another's lives. "I have people I can trust, people I like and who like me, but they aren't real friends."

Differing expectations and definitions of friendship lead easily to painful cross cultural confusion. Brazilians and other cultural groups, like Saudi Arabians,[7] often feel that American overtures of friendship are insincere, "like a permanent smile," according to one Brazilian. A standard bit of advice given to Brazilians embarking for the United States is "Don't mistake courtesy for friendship." The initial interest and concern a North American shows a foreigner, coupled with an informal approach to acquaintanceship and the sharing of personal concerns that many foreigners consider quite intimate, create an expectation of friendship that is not maintained in subsequent actions. The American goes about his business, assuming the foreigner will ask for help if he needs it, while the foreigner feels deserted and alone. A Brazilian woman told of encountering a bad case of the flu shortly after her arrival in the United States. She was amazed that her new-found American friends seemed unconcerned and uninterested in her health. She felt they had abandoned her. In the same situation, Brazilians would flock to the sick person to help, to express their concern, "to the point that the sick person may not, in fact, get the rest he needs." Only later did she learn that her North American friends assumed she would rather be alone to recover and that she would certainly ask for help if she needed it. Further, social mechanisms that Americans see as signs of personal regard (like the sending of flowers or the mailing of greeting cards, for example) strike Brazilians as impersonal and as a way of avoiding personal, human contact.

Privacy

The Brazilian concept of privacy strikes the American sometimes as contradictory and often as bewildering. The extended family living situation, the general concern for the group rather than the individual, and an appreciation for the human world around them, all create situations in which Brazilians are rarely alone. A person who wants to be alone is assumed to be sad, and most Brazilians we questioned were hard pressed to think of times when they were regularly alone. As described in detail below, Brazilians feel much freer to express themselves conversationally, through comments and questions, and physically, through hugging, kissing, standing close, and the like. Such factors lead Americans to think that Brazilians have little sense of privacy, and certainly Americans do seem to have a more exclusive sense of privacy than do Brazilians. However, to say that Brazilians have no sense of privacy is far from accurate.

Little privacy exists between family members, and little exists between friends, between *amigos*. Between *colegas*, a greater degree exists, and until one enters the relationship of a *colega*, Brazilians can be very private people indeed. As one Brazilian summarized the differences between Brazilians and Americans: "We are warmer toward those we know, but less trustful of a stranger." The issue is more complex than just one of degree, involving striking differences between what Brazilians and Americans consider to be private matters. Home and family are very private matters to a Brazilian. One should not ask a Brazilian about family life, marital status, or related subjects unless the other specifically mentions them first. One should not drop in unannounced at a Brazilian home, and one should probably not telephone before being told such a call would be appropriate or being given the home telephone number. Brazilian upper and upper-middle-class homes often sit behind a high fence, a solid and tangible proof of the separation a Brazilian wants to maintain between his family and the world at large. One American anthropologist lived for a year in Brazil before being invited into a colleague's home for dinner. He was frequently entertained in restaurants and bars, which allowed his Brazilian hosts to get to know him and, later, allowed their wives to meet him also, but only after a great deal of such socializing was he invited into a Brazilian home. The initial visit to a Brazilian home might be accomplished in the garden or yard adjacent to the house, or in a living room or den inside the house, but not necessarily in the midst of family life. Americans often misinterpret this privacy accorded to home and family as unfriendliness or as a negative judgment against themselves. It is neither, and being entertained outside the home in a bar or being taken to dinner at a restaurant is considered a friendly and hospitable way to get acquainted with a stranger or better acquainted with an associate.

Time and Order

A major component of the outsider's stereotype of Latin Americans is that "they are always late." One component of the Brazilian stereotype of Americans is that "you are always prompt." Like all stereotypes, neither statement is completely true, though each statement contains a germ of truth. Bus and train schedules in Rio and São Paulo are closely followed. However, in some areas of Brazil, television programs are scheduled by sequence rather than by the hour or half hour. Though most Americans consider themselves punctual, especially in relation to other cultures, most Americans have friends and acquaintances who are habitually late. Both stereotypes stem from and reflect two very different views of the world. Edward T. Hall has named these different views according to the manner in which each organizes time. Monochronic time or M-time typifies most Americans, who tend to concentrate on one thing at a time and so to schedule events individually, thus we divide time into small units and are concerned with promptness (a ten-minute margin may be too lax in some situations). Polychronic or P-time typifies most Latin Americans and most Brazilians, though places like São Paulo are, through the demands of industrialization, becoming more M-time oriented. P-time organization does not divide time into small units or concern itself with tight schedules. P-time systems, according to Hall, "are characterized by several things happening at once. They stress involvement of people and completion of transactions rather than adherence to present schedules. P-time is treated as much less tangible than M-time."[8] One study comparing perceptions of punctuality in the United States and Brazil found that Brazilian timepieces were less reliable and public clocks less available than in the United States. Researchers also found that Brazilians more often described themselves as late arrivers, allowed greater flexibility in defining early and late, were less concerned about being late, and were more likely to blame external factors for their lateness than were Americans interviewed and tested. Despite these contrasts, "Brazilians do not see themselves as people who do not care about punctuality. They do not share the stereotyped American view of themselves as people who wish to delay everything until *amanhã.*"⁹ The authors continue to describe the Brazilian attitude as more flexible rather than less punctual.

The contrast between the two systems shows most obviously in the American attempts to schedule and subsequent frustration with the Brazilian lack of concern for that schedule. The American interprets this lack of concern as a lack of interest in himself, in the matter at hand, or as a more general indifference toward "getting things done." Brazilians, too, are frustrated by the situation, and do not understand how Americans can place more importance on an abstract schedule than on human beings with human needs that may not meet the constraints of that schedule. One Brazilian who ran afoul of the American obsession for time described her hosts as acting "like I was a machine that could not fail." To a Brazilian, "British time," "Swiss time," and "American time" mean "Be prompt!" While Americans may not, in fact, be as prompt as they like to imagine themselves to be, they do perceive themselves as prompt and perceive promptness as a virtue. The study of punctuality mentioned above found that North Americans equated promptness with success—the more punctual a person is, the more successful he or she will be. "This trend was reversed for Brazilians, for whom arriving late was a badge of success."¹⁰

Doing Favors

These contrasting perceptions and values show clearly in contrasting attitudes regarding the doing of favors. Most Americans prefer to do things themselves if possible, the general attitude being that one should avoid "owing" favors and that if a favor is done, it should be repaid. We feel no qualms about being unable to perform a favor and consider such matters as doctor appointments or studying for an exam legitimate excuses that should neither hurt nor offend the asker.

Brazilians often ask favors of friends, especially of close friends, but also of acquaintances. Jon Tolman points out that favors "are mechanisms for validating *colega* and *amigo* status. That is why they are *so* important. Also, a favor must be done personally or refused. Brazilians understand a refusal, but are angered by the typical American response of telling someone else to do it."[11] Brazilians also share a different concept of just what constitutes a favor. Small things not requiring much responsibility or time are not considered favors, but just part of normal interaction. The request for a favor might be in the form of an indirect hint rather than a direct question, and many Brazilians are hesitant to ask unless they feel fairly sure they can be accommodated. Likewise, most Brazilians will perform a favor when asked rather than refuse a request. A job might be a legitimate excuse to refuse a favor, but a doctor's appointment could easily be changed; one Brazilian told of borrowing money to lend to another friend rather than saying "No." When a Brazilian cannot perform a favor, several possible responses eliminate the need for a direct refusal. "I might say, 'I have a test, but if you can't find someone else, call me.'" "I would suggest other friends to do the favor." Some Brazilians find saying no more difficult than performing a favor, and so will do the favor "even if they are angry about it." A standard comment on such a situation is *"Você dá um jeito"* or *"Você dá um jeitinho."* The phrase defies easy English translation. Literally, *jeito* means a skill. It is used when Americans might say, "We'll find a way to work it out." Brazilians dislike the American refusal of "I'd love to but. . .," and one Brazilian woman observed that she finds herself making excuses for North Americans beforehand, "So I won't feel so bad when they say 'No.'" Because the concern for human feelings and human relations makes the refusing of favors difficult, some Brazilians may agree to do a favor even though circumstances make their performance of it impossible. Knowing this, Brazilians might ask several friends for the same favor, so that one, at least, should be able to comply.

Brazilians do not "balance" favors as Americans often do, and so Brazilians do not feel obligated to repay a favor immediately. Depending upon the amount of time and trouble a person has taken, a Brazilian might do something nice as a gesture of appreciation, but too marked an insistence on repaying might give offense. Brazilians do, however, feel freer to ask favors of those they have done favors for in the past. "Someday, you might need my help." "Later on, I'll do something for you. It will work out."

Such attitudes make the act of borrowing a potentially tricky business, and a traditional proverb warns that "you should never loan three things: your books, your money, or your wife."

Brazilians do borrow items and goods from one another fairly regularly, and the closer the relationship, the freer one is to borrow. As with favors generally, saying no to a request to borrow poses problems. Rarely will the response be a direct "No." To protect the feelings of the potential borrower, and to extricate himself from the situation graciously, a Brazilian "would always explain, give reasons, excuses." Some examples: "It's not mine;" "It's a family heirloom;" "My grandmother would be upset;" "This necklace, I'm so jealous of it I wouldn't lend it to my sister." Likewise, asking for the return of a borrowed object is difficult. "You don't want to seem greedy by asking for something back. You behave almost like it didn't belong to you." A Brazilian might try to borrow the same thing from someone else, to avoid asking for the return of a borrowed item. "If I did ask, I would say, 'I need it. Could I give it back to you if you still need it when I'm done?'" "I would maneuver the subject into the conversation." A Brazilian would ask directly only as a last resort, yet that is probably the first thing an American would do.

Two Views, One World

The contrast between systems reaches much further than the making, breaking, or delaying of appointments. It is a result of the coming together of the basic North American personality, which emphasizes the individual, set goals, competition between individuals to meet goals, and a general tendency to look to the future, and the "basic Brazilian personality, which stresses direct personal relations, based on liking rather than on unconditional, impersonal, practical relations."[12] If North Americans see Brazilians as casual regarding work and time, Brazilians see North Americans as distant regarding their human environment. Brazilians admire the public order they see in the United States, where technology and industrialization have made the country and the individuals in it independent and self-sufficient. Public support systems in Brazil tend to be less efficient, particularly in smaller towns. Phones might not work well, power failures are not unusual, garbage collection is irregular. At the same time, "people are happier and more carefree." Brazilians often do not have the myriad machines and appliances that Americans have. Instead, maids often serve people. While the lack of technology may mean that jobs take longer to perform, it also means that one interacts "with human beings. Americans have a need for self-sufficiency, have your own, do it yourself, won't ask for help, always in a hurry to be alone." Organization can create distance, as "looking through a cardboard tube narrows vision."[13] As one Brazilian commented, "People are never doing nothing in North America. You always have something specific to do. In Brazil, more people do nothing, just walk, have a drink in a bar."

An interesting example of the contrasting value systems is a Brazilian gesture called *vida boa*, the good life (cf. Independent Gestures, figure 54). When asked what the gesture meant, Brazilians replied, "It's joking; it means someone is lazy." Later, other interviewees explained the gesture as indicating "someone is successful." We, in typical monochronic fashion, were confused by what we perceived as the incongruities of success and laziness. Further probing brought forth the explanation that success means a person can relax and enjoy the good life—a very different interpretation of success from that of many Americans, for whom "success permits no letdown or release except through failure."[14] Another nonverbal cue to the Brazilian character stems from the existence of several different gestures that indicate "more or less," "so-so," "it's not important," (cf. page 108, figures 43–45). These gestures (particularly the brushing together of the fingertips) were, in our observation, the most frequently used of all we recorded. The group of gestures reflects a relaxed approach to the world and to problems in it and a willingness to take things as they are, attitudes not particularly common in North America.

One finds less competition for jobs in Brazil, where many jobs are gained through friends and family connections, and people are frequently judged on personal standards rather than abstract (i.e., prompt, efficient) or job-specific (i.e., typing, previous experience) qualities. Brazilians do not highly regard ambition as do Americans and may view an ambitious person as one who tries to keep others down for his own benefit. The means to the end are very important to a Brazilian, who will probably seek a very different goal from the American in any case. Americans value directness, whereas Latin Americans, because of the value placed on human relations and comfortable interaction, often approach a subject or a problem indirectly, working toward a solution by degrees. The American often wants to move straight to the major

issue, to find a permanent solution and to find it fast. One analyst
of Brazilian culture, José Honório Rodrigues, offers the following
summary:

> The basic Luso-Brazilian personality has a horror of
> violence and always seeks a way of smoothing things
> over, a path of moderation that avoids definite breaks.
> Cleverness, prudence in shunning extremes, an ability to
> forget, a rich sense of humor, a cool head, and a warm
> heart get the Brazilians through difficult moments.[15]

This concern for smoothing things over has marked Brazilian
history as relatively peaceful, characterized by "conciliation
rather than revolution."[16] The same concern for smoothing things
over marks daily life, meaning that business deals, job recom-
mendations, or the asking of a favor might all be approached
slowly and indirectly. Rodrigues notes that an 1850's traveler's
account of Brazil observed the same characteristic, that "Nothing
was done with haste, and the words, 'Be patient' were among the
most frequently heard by those who had to endure the eternal
postponement of solutions to their problems."[17]

Brazilians regard an indirect approach as gracious and as a
way of sparing the other's feelings, a way to avoid putting the
other on the spot, in a potentially awkward situation. The
American regards the same approach as inefficient and as a way
of evading the issue. The American is frustrated by the Brazilian
lack of concern and sees it as a refusal to face facts. The Brazilian
is hurt and dismayed by the American's bluntness and perceives
it as a disregard for the human feelings involved with those facts.
As noted earlier, Brazilians call their approach to solving a
problem *dar um jeito* or *dar um jeitinho*, and the problems
requiring *jeito* can range from performing a difficult favor for a
friend to getting a driver's license or a passport (fraught with
bureaucratic red tape in Brazil) and from negotiating a tricky
business deal to getting a car repaired. "There's always a way to
work it out," said one Brazilian when asked about performing a
difficult favor. "There is always a way of arranging things" said
another.

This pervasive attitude aptly summarizes Brazilian world
view, particularly since the "arranging" nearly always weighs
personal chemistry and human relations over more or less
concrete facts and mechanical processes. Whether one offers a

higher price to speed a process along or attempts to elicit a lower price from a vendor in a *feira*, whether one is an employer asking for a letter of recommendation or a potential employee looking for a job, one must always consider the personal relations involved in a situation. To ignore those relations is to invite delay, frustration, and often failure in communicating with Brazilians.

Notes

1. Charles Wagley, *An Introduction to Brazil* (New York: Columbia Univ. Press, 1963; rev. ed. 1971), pp. 142–43.

2. Florestan Fernandes, "The Negro in Brazilian Society: Twenty-five Years Later," *Brazil: Anthropological Perspectives. Essays in Honor of Charles Wagley.* Maxine L. Margolis & Werleiani E. Custer, Eds. (New York: Columbia Univ. Press, 1979), p. 108.

3. Fernandes, p. 112.

4. José Honório Rodrigues, *The Brazilians: Their Character and Aspirations*, Ralph Edward Dimmick, trans. (Austin: Univ. of Texas Press, 1967), p. 94.

5. Wagley, p. 168.

6. Charles Wagley, *The Latin-American Tradition: Essays on the Unity and Diversity of Latin-American Culture* (New York: Columbia Univ. Press, 1968), p. 57.

7. Sahnny Johnson, personal communication.

8. Edward T. Hall, *Beyond Culture* (Garden City, New York: Anchor Press/Doubleday, 1976), p. 14ff.

9. Robert V. Levine, Laurie J. West, and Harry T. Reis, "Perceptions of Time and Punctuality in the United States and Brazil," *Journal of Personality and Social Psychology* 38 (1980), p. 549.

10. Levine et al., "Perceptions of Time," p. 550.

11. Jon Tolman, University of New Mexico, personal communication, November 17, 1981.

12. Rodrigues, *The Brazilians*, p. 57.

13. Hall, *Beyond Culture*, p. 17.

14. Alexander Lowen, *The Betrayal of the Body* (New York: Macmillan, 1967), p. 16.

15. Rodrigues, *The Brazilians*, p. 59.

16. Rodrigues, *The Brazilians*, p. 59.

17. Rodrigues, *The Brazilians*, p. 50.

CONVERSATIONAL CONCERNS

On Touching

The observation that Latin Americans show great appreciation for close proximity and body contact has become commonplace, and most Americans are aware that while in Latin America they should expect to be much closer to others than they are used to being. Alfred Hower suggests that "Americans talking to each other stand at least a foot further back."[1] Brazilians are no exception to the general Latin rule, and in fact "have a reputation for touching a lot" even among Latins.

In crowded public places, like an elevator, a bus, or a Saturday morning *feira* (open market), Brazilians stand closer to one another than a North American expects, and do not apologize for bumping or brushing against another person. North Americans give themselves away by what strikes a Brazilian as a constant stream of "excuse me" and "pardon me" when negotiating through a crowd. In places like banks or supermarkets, customers form lines, as in the United States, but stand much closer to other people in line than would a North American. Also, while people often try to enter the head of the line, others behind protest loudly. In places like a public market, lines rarely form and the buyer must push (and sometimes literally elbow) his way to the front of the booth. One woman from Bahia reported receiving funny looks from North Americans when, in typical Brazilian fashion, she placed her hands on a stranger's arms to move herself gently by him. Such touching needs no apology in Brazil.

The Brazilian inclination toward touching shows dramatically (or at least, shows dramatically to a North American) during conversation. A Brazilian man may put an arm around another's shoulders, pat or poke his back or tummy, or perhaps squeeze his shoulder, sometimes in greeting, sometimes to emphasize a point, and sometimes just as a gesture of goodwill and friendship (figures 1 and 2). Brazilian men as a rule touch less frequently than do women or children, and touching between

Figure 1
Male conversational posture
and body contact

Figure 2
Male conversational
posture and body contact

men tends to be of shorter duration. For instance, a Brazilian man
might greet another with a slap on the back, and might leave his
hand on the other's back or his arm or around his shoulder for a
moment while walking the space of a few yards. He would
probably not, however, walk any great distance or remain
standing more than a moment with his arm around the other's
shoulders.

Women tend to touch more than men, and adolescents, both
male and female, touch more than adults. One Brazilian explained this in an interesting way by saying "Your hands grow
more during the teen years, so you need to have your hands on
something." Young women may walk with arms around one
another, with arms linked, or holding hands (figures 3 and 4) and
many Brazilians have stories ranging from amused to embarrassed to pained concerning the North American equation of such
behavior with homosexuality or lesbianism. Young women
might, during conversation, curl another's hair around a finger,

Figure 3
Female conversational
posture and body contact

Figure 4
Female conversational
posture and body contact

tug at jewelry, shirt collar or buttons, or might fiddle with the other's hand. One woman described buttoning and unbuttoning the top button of her sister's shirt as they talked.

A Brazilian who feels his companion's attention is wandering might grab the other's chin to redirect his gaze, or might tug the other's arm or lightly strike his leg to get his attention. A young woman who has taught in the United States tells of surprising her students by patting them on the shoulder or back. Most touching occurs between peers, so a younger person would probably not touch an older person in these informal ways, nor would strangers touch so. Most touching occurs between members of the same sex (one of the things Americans find disturbing), though an older male acquaintance might give a fatherly pat on the arm to a young girl.

Many Brazilians feel that Americans have substituted words for actions, that an American must articulate what the Brazilian can demonstrate. This substitution leads to a proliferation, in Brazilian eyes, of empty and cliched phrases like "Have a nice day!" or "Take care!" that allow the speaker to express a courtesy but to avoid involvement. Brazilians often feel uncomfortable when the obvious or the emotional is directly expressed in words and tend to relay emotional information through touch. The clearest example of the differences might be young couples who, in Brazil, display affection frequently and publicly by walking with arms around each other, kissing, embracing, holding hands, and gazing into one another's eyes. John B. Jensen submitted the following anecdote of Brazilian couple behavior:

> I know of a young American girl being "hustled" by a *carioca* boy, who insisted on kissing her passionately on a crowded rushhour bus. She resisted, pointing out all the people watching them. His very Brazilian response: "Close your eyes."[2]

Brazilians looking at Americans "can't tell who's friends and who's a couple." Further, whereas Americans equate touching directly with sexual involvement, Brazilians equate touching with general friendship and concern.

Eye Contact

Just as Brazilians touch one another more than do North Americans, so do they look at one another more than do North Americans. In crowded places like an elevator, where North Americans tend to gaze straight ahead, or on a bus, where North Americans look out a window, straight ahead, or at the floor, Brazilians look around them and at one another. If eyes meet, individuals might be a trifle embarrassed but would probably smile and perhaps initiate a quick, casual conversation. Though women do not engage eye contact with or respond to conversational overtures from a strange man, a certain amount of eye contact with strangers is expected, and one who obviously avoids eye contact will probably arouse curiosity. If Brazilians don't want to look at the people around them they will probably look at the ground. During conversation, eye contact is maintained between both speaker and listener to a degree that Americans often consider a stare. Americans tend to maintain intermittent rather than sustained eye contact during a conversation, where each party looks at the other briefly and then away briefly, and so find the steady Brazilian gaze disconcerting. One exception among Brazilians is when people of different age or status converse, particularly if the higher-status, more powerful person is in any way reprimanding the other. Then, the less powerful person generally looks down and away from the more powerful one. This downcast gaze is a sign of lower/less powerful status, and is not, as Americans sometimes interpret it, a sign of evasiveness or deceit. Brazilians, like Americans, associate a steady gaze with sincerity. Consequently, "If a Brazilian is going to lie in such a situation, he will look you straight in the eye and swear on his or her mother, etc."

Style and Topics

Brazilians enjoy conversation and, as was noted earlier, might strike up a conversation with people in places where an American might not. Further, Brazilians are always ready to stop for a conversation with friends, wherever they might meet. Whereas Brazilians find Americans more courteous in public places like supermarkets, pushing or jostling less and excusing themselves more, they also find Americans less receptive to friends in the same situation. "Going [grocery] shopping is a very individual thing . . . here. Brazilians are receptive to friends whenever, wherever they meet, will talk and talk, might even forget what they came to buy." Conversations tend to be much more animated between Brazilians than between North Americans, and this animation results in seemingly contradictory judgments, with each group labelling the other as "loud." Brazilians do let their emotions show through tone, volume, and the use of gestures, believing that one ought to vent one's feelings for one's own sake and for the sake of others. Brazilians in a group not only talk loudly to one another, but often also all talk at once. "It's not rude. They're all listening too." Hence, while interrupting is considered rude in formal conversation, it happens frequently in informal conversation, where it is considered part of the normal manner of discourse and even, perhaps, a mark of enthusiasm. Brazilians find the North American tendency to "keep cool," to maintain an unruffled appearance, frustrating and confusing. "They are only half people. You are what you express." Brazilians also feel that, while they are noisy in conversation with others, North American often make themselves conspicuous by loud behavior in public—shouting at others across a room or through a crowd, being loud just for the sake of being loud. One Brazilian remarked that "the only time North Americans are loud is on weekends and when they are drunk."

Strictures concerning what can and cannot be talked about differ as much as the manner in which the two cultures converse.

Brazilians enjoy joking and teasing, and men in particular enjoy the double entendre. They also tend to be quite candid regarding personal characteristics and physical traits, commenting upon and asking questions about things a North American would probably notice but ignore. One Brazilian woman told of her dislike for the constant questions asked by other Brazilians concerning scars she had received in an accident. A Brigham Young University study gives several examples:

Are you fat? Are you skinny? Do you have any other physical characteristics about which you are sensitive? If so, be prepared for the candid reactions of Brazilians to your distinguishing feature. They will have no compunction about saying something like, "You really have a lot of pimples, John. You ought to have that taken care of." In speaking of another person, they may say, "Do you know Mr. Oliveira, the fat one?" People in Brazil don't intend such remarks to be insulting or offensive, but speak of traits like obesity as naturally as if they were referring to blond hair or blue eyes.[3]

One North American exchange student noticed that Brazilians would talk about her in the third person while she was present, making such comments as "Isn't she cute?" Her exchange family would notice any change in her physical appearance, and she interpreted comments like "Don't you want to wash your hair?" or "My, haven't you gained weight!" as observations only, not criticism. These American interpretations are accurate to a degree, but Jon Tolman of the University of New Mexico points out that in some situations, questions like "Don't you want to wash your hair?" are part of a more comprehensive Brazilian pattern which uses hints and indirection to accomplish a goal. "Brazilians would consider our American directness rude, and the Brazilian habit of asking leading questions often leads to Americans not getting the point. . . . When you are in a Brazilian home and the hostess says innocently, 'My, you must be tired,' or some such, she is really hinting you should go home." Tolman also sees the matter of candor regarding personal traits as reflecting a deep cultural difference between Brazilians and Americans. He notes that Brazilians sometimes base a nickname on a deformity, as with the nineteenth century sculptor afflicted with leprosy and known as *Aleijadinho* or Little Cripple. "By doing so, the 'defect' is desensitized, objectified, and less apt to be traumatic. . . . Americans hide these things, will not acknowledge them, and so they become the basis for neurosis."[4]

At the same time, Brazilians are surprised by the amount of personal information Americans volunteer upon a relatively short acquaintance, things a Brazilian would discuss only with a friend or long-term acquaintance. One should be careful discussing topics involving sex and should avoid obscene jokes or any topics directly involving obscenity when in mixed company. Women discuss boyfriends, but do not discuss living with a boyfriend, a phenomenon growing more common but still likely to be a touchy subject in Brazil. Age, too, should be avoided. "If you're over eighteen, you're an adult. That's all that counts. Here it's the second thing you ask. 'What's your name? How old are you?' " One should not ask about another's marital status, particularly if it seems the other party might be separated or divorced. One's family is considered very important and very private, and not a topic for conversation with a new acquaintance. However, if one does know a member of the family, courtesy demands that his health be inquired after.

Finally, Brazilians are excellent conversationalists. Most are expert at the art North Americans call "small talk." The overwhelming concern for social relations, for human relations on a daily basis, that is basic to Brazilian culture kindles a genuine interest in one's fellow man. When a Brazilian makes a new acquaintance, he avoids the subjects mentioned earlier but pursues many others, so that even Brazilians describe themselves as "curious." The educational system in Brazil encourages students to develop their own ideas by questioning the ideas of others, so from a fairly early age, Brazilians are trained to express their opinions and to argue for them, whether or not they have a specific authority behind them. Most middle and upper-classs Brazilians are quite knowledgeable about national and international affairs and enjoy discussing both. Finally, Brazilians enjoy rhetoric for its own sake. José Honório Rodrigues's study of Brazilian national character summarizes the North American and Brazilian attitudes thus:

> In the United States and England, . . . there is an excess of words and a liking for rhetoric, but rhetoric is clearly recognized as such. In these latter countries, rhetoric is rhetoric, and it offers no solutions. In Brazil, rhetoric is an integral part of thought and is presented as a solution.

Verbalization, as Rodrigues labels this characteristic, may sometimes result in "a confusion of words with deeds," but certainly results in skilled talkers who value the spoken word. While a less verbal culture, like the Japanese, might find North Americans to be good conversationalists, a highly verbal culture, like Brazil's, does not.[7] Brazilians often find North Americans sparsely informed on international affairs, not to mention Brazilian affairs, and find them not particularly skilled at the witty, teasing banter typical of much Brazilian interaction. The tendency of Americans to enumerate various points in an argument strikes Brazilians as overly pedantic. American women are noted for their difficulty in accepting a compliment, a basis of male-female interaction in Brazil.

Greetings and Introductions

Differences between Brazilian and North American manners of greeting are marked. Brazilians feel that North Americans do not greet one another much at all, and that such greeting as does take place either tends to be very formal or rather superficial. They note a lack of physical contact which bespeaks formality and distance, and as mentioned earlier, they note a proliferation of such cliches as "Have a nice day!" exchanged indiscriminately between relative strangers and close friends. "In America, the more you know someone, the less you greet them. In Brazil, the reverse is true. The friendlier people are with each other, the more they greet each other." Certainly, North Americans have few specific rules regarding the greeting of friends and acquaintances. Brazilians do not have a great many such customs, but those they have are important and frequently used. A Brazilian would not think of passing a friend or acquaintance without giving a greeting. Even people one knows by sight rather than personally, like neighbors in an apartment complex or people one sees regularly going to and from work, ought to be acknowledged. Just how one greets an individual depends upon the strength of the relationship. In the case of people one knows only by sight, a nod, smile, or simple phrase is sufficient, but if one knows the individual at all, something more will probably be expected.

A formal or business-like introduction is often accompanied by a handshake, particularly between men. The hand is grasped firmly and is usually held for a longer period of time than is the

North American custom. A Brazilian might grasp the other's hand in both of his own, to indicate a particularly warm greeting, or he might grasp the other's forearm with the left hand. The handshake is usually also accompanied by mutual eye contact and smiles, and perhaps by a mutual nod. If two men are well acquainted, the handshake might be accompanied by a slap on the shoulder, on the stomach, or a sustained patting on the back, and might last through the greeting and even into the conversation. Brazilian women being introduced for the first time or in a formal situation are also likely to shake hands, though they might simply nod to acknowledge the introduction. As a gesture of greeting or farewell, or during a conversation, Brazilians exchange handshakes. When joining or leaving a group of people, a Brazilian shakes the hand of each person. Shaking the hand of the nearest person and giving an inclusive wave to the rest would be rude by Brazilian standards. A North American told of a Brazilian friend who saw him at a ballgame and, not satisfied with a wave, walked through several rows of spectators to shake his hand. The North American admitted rather ruefully that, were he to return to Brazil, he would make a genuine effort to shake hands with friends and acquaintances on every occasion. "If you're carrying things, put them down." If one's hands are dirty, the forearm can · be offered to the other person who will grasp it warmly. As a Brazilian woman observed, "It's the contact that's important." One study summarizes the custom of handshaking thus:

> Shaking hands is a common practice in Brazil. Brazilians shake hands at the slightest opportunity: when they meet people, when they see friends or say goodby to them, even when these are people they see everyday. Their shaking hands is less formal and warmer than is customarily the case in the United States and it is often followed by a slight *abraço* [hug].[8]

An informal, friendly handshake between men is very warm, and the hug or embrace that may accompany it is not necessarily slight by North American standards. One North American who has spent much time in Brazil describes it as a "bear hug" (figure 5). The only time Brazilians might not shake hands upon being introduced is when the introduction takes place across the dinner or lunch table, in which case a nod and a smile is sufficient acknowledgement.

The most common greeting used between women is the kiss, generally given more than once—usually twice and sometimes three times—on alternate cheeks. A traditional custom for determining how many kisses to exchange is to give married women two kisses and single women three, and one might say "Give me three so I'll be married," or "Give me three, so I won't be an old maid." A bit more complicated expression comes from a woman from Rio, where a passing trend encouraged, for a brief time, the exchange of five kisses: *"Três prá casar; quatro prá não brigar com a sogra; cinco prá não ter filho bicha."* Translation: "Three times so you get married; four times so you won't fight with your mother-in-law; five times os you won't have a gay son." The expression is more generally known as *"Três prá casar; quatro pra não morar com a sogra."* The kiss may not involve an actual kiss on the cheek, although it certainly may. Often women brush cheeks while kissing the air (figures 6 and 7). In a more formal situation, women might not actually brush cheeks, and sometimes a perfunctory swinging of the head over each shoulder takes the place of the kiss/brush of the cheek. One usually begins the gesture with a movement to the left and with contact between righthand cheeks.

Figure 5
Male *abraço*

Figure 6
Female kiss of greeting; cheeks touch

Figure 7
Female kiss of greeting; cheeks do not touch

The kiss as greeting is used to say hello, to take leave of a friend or acquaintance, and sometimes to acknowledge an introduction. It may be used between women who are related, good friends, acquaintances, or even strangers, and Brazilians see it as the equivalent of the handshake, as often "just a courtesy." A woman always greets a female friend with a kiss, and even if the meeting was opened with a handshake between strangers, it is likely to be closed with a kiss. This greeting was traditionally exchanged only between women, though over the past years, the single and double kiss has come to be used between men and women also, especially among the younger people. If a man gives a woman a kiss of greeting, he generally only kisses one cheek. Most often, Brazilian men shake hands, pat the back, and give an embrace/bear hug as described earlier, though a father might kiss his son. A kiss on the lips is usually romantic in Brazil. Parents and older relatives to whom one shows love and respect are greeted by a single kiss on the cheek, never by a kiss on the lips, and when joining or leaving family visits and family celebrations, everyone kisses everyone. The rules covering who to kiss and how many times to kiss are not clear cut, and Brazilians themselves find many situations confusing. One can always wait for the other party to initiate the greeting, though this may not help to ease the Brazilian stereotype of North Americans as cold and distant. Women should at the very least be prepared to kiss and to be kissed, knowing that such is a standard Brazilian courtesy.

Except in formal situations, introductions tend to be quite casual in Brazil. Introductions are not considered obligatory when friends meet or when a newcomer joins a group, and when individuals are introduced, generally only the first names are used. First and last names are not used much in conversation or introductions, but as one woman observed, "You don't need to be known by name to be a part of the group." Introductions might make a Brazilian uncomfortable by imparting a degree of formality to a gathering. Brazilians may not know an acquaintance's surname, and even in the business world, when an American would use "Mr. Smith," a Brazilian would likely use "Senhor Angelo." John Jensen provides more specific information on name usage in Brazil:

> School teachers, even college professors, are usually known only by their first names, or by title and first name: Tia Sueli (elementary school), Professor Carlos, Mestre Francisco (rare), Doutor Antônio. The same can be said for other professionals, such as priests (Padre João) and nuns (Irmã Fátima), physicians (Doutor Guilherme), etc. This is particularly true in the northeast and interior areas, but it also occurs in the cities. Exceptions seem to be a matter of an individual's formality: some people just come across as Senhor Vargas or Doutor Chagas. When the last name is used, the first name may be virtually unknown outside the family. Occasionally first and last names are both used, and may become so fused that one is not used without the others, such as with the linguist Celso Cunha, who I have never heard referred to as either Celso or Cunha, at least among students and professionals.
>
> It is still the custom to maintain lists and files alphabetized by the first name, rather than by last name, although the telephone directories in most cities now use the last name. The concept of "last name first" on all American forms strikes Brazilians as odd, as does the insistence of acquaintances on knowing and using the last name, not to speak of institutions that may virtually create new identities for Brazilians based on a last name that may have been little used in Brazil.[9]

The final name of a signature is usually the surname. Many Brazilians retain their mother's name. Some women retain their mother's name, drop the father's name, and add the husband's name upon marriage. Though Brazilian women, as of 1977, are no longer required by law to change their names upon marriage, most do take the husband's name. Brazilian tags indicating junior or son (*filho*), and III or grandson (*neto*), are part of a man's legal signature, but are not used as part of the spoken name.

Notes

1. Alfred Hower, University of Florida, personal communication, November 3, 1981.
2. John B. Jensen, Florida International University, personal communication, November 17, 1981.
3. *People of Brazil* (Provo, Utah: Brigham Young Univ., Language and Intercultural Research Center, 1977), p. 16.
4. Jon M. Tolman, University of New Mexico, personal communication, November 17, 1981.
5. José Honório Rodrigues, *The Brazilians: Their Characters and Aspirations*, Ralph Edward Dimmick, trans. (Austin: Univ. of Texas Press, 1967), p. 47.
6. Rodrigues, *The Brazilians*, p. 50.
7. Observations concerning Japanese culture: Sahnny Johnson, personal communication, September 16, 1981.
8. Maria Isabel Abreu and Cléa Rameh, *Português Contemporâneo I* (Washington, D.C.: Georgetown Univ., 1972), pp. 11–12.
9. John B. Jensen, personal communication, November 17, 1981.

FOOD and EATING

North Americans proclaim their presence by the way they eat. Many Brazilians are surprised, if not shocked, by standard North American eating habits. The first observation offered by Brazilians when asked how North Americans eat was, "Oh you Americans, you eat with your hands!" And we do eat a number of things with our hands—fruit, sandwiches, chicken, pizza—for which a Brazilian would use utensils. Fruit is generally peeled and sliced, and if not served in a dish is sliced as it is eaten. Bananas, when they are cooked and served with a meal, are slit open and the pulp scraped from the skin with a fork, though uncooked bananas are eaten as North Americans eat them. Sandwiches, if served on a plate, are eaten with a knife and fork. If they are held in the hand, they are wrapped in a napkin, so that the hands do not touch the sandwich itself. Generally, food that is held in the hand is wrapped in this way. Utensils are used for meats, even chicken. Several Brazilians told anecdotes of their first trips to North American pizza parlors, where they had to ask for knives and forks, always used with Brazilian pizza. Aside from the general concern of not eating with the hands, Brazilian pizza is very different from the North American variety, often having a thick and crumbly crust, and sliced or mashed tomatoes rather than tomato sauce. Brazilian bread, similar to French bread, is an exception and can be eaten with the hands, usually by breaking off small portions of the loaf. During a formal dinner, one should not butter an entire slice of bread, but only the portion one is about to eat. The safest rule concerning hands and food is to use the hands as little as possible and to observe the Brazilians around you. Using the hands to eat is, by Brazilian standards, unhygienic and ill-mannered.

Another North American habit that strikes Brazilians as odd and perhaps rude is eating in public, particularly eating while walking on the street. Young people might eat fruit, ice cream, or candy while walking, but eating on the street generally suggests immaturity and/or poor manners. Street stands and *barzinhos* (informal street cafes or bars) may have tables or counters at which one can eat; if not, one should stand nearby and eat rather than walk away eating a sandwich or drinking. Some Brazilians feel uncomfortable eating in a place like the typical student cafeteria, where one is surrounded by numbers of people and various activities. "Americans bring their lunches, eat in front of everyone. The talk just goes on. You feel funny, to have your mouth full, to have to talk."

Part of the hesitancy to eat in public or in front of others who are not eating stems from the Brazilian attitude that food should always be shared. If a visitor arrives during a meal, he will be invited to join. If a friend approaches another who is eating something, the person eating will offer a portion, whatever it might be. A cookie could be broken in half; a sandwich could be passed for a bite. Even if the amount of food involved is clearly not sufficient to share, the offer *(O Senhor é servido?* or simply *A Senhora é servida?)* should be made. Because a Brazilian extends his hospitality no matter how inconvenient, one generally refuses the first offer with *obrigado/a* (thanks). That way the person eating can show his generosity without risking the embarrassment of insufficient food. The offer will probably be extended again, at which time the other person or persons may accept, taking a small portion if the item you are being offered is in short supply. If the refusal is intended as firm, one should offer an excuse or an explanation, so that the offerer is not offended. When accepting an offer, one must say "Yes" or "Please." "Thank you" indicates a refusal in Brazil, where "No, thank you" is rudely blunt.

Brazilian breakfast is usually small, consisting of bread and butter, juice, sometimes fruit, and nearly always *café com leite*, coffee with milk. The latter uses more milk than coffee (in some cases it is made with milk rather than with water) and is sweetened with sugar. *Café preto*, black coffee, or *cafezinho*, little coffee, means a strong, darkly roasted coffee without milk but with lots of sugar. Traditionally, lunch is the largest meal of the day, and many Brazilians still maintain this pattern despite the eight-to-five routine demanded by increasing industrialization. Some businesses close for two hours at noon so that employees have time to go home for the midday meal, extending the work day to six o'clock.

A traditional lunch would include *arroz e feijão* (rice and beans) and meat. *Feijoada* is a standard Brazilian dish, traditionally served on Wednesdays and Saturdays. It consists of highly spiced black beans cooked with a variety of meats and is eaten with rice. Beans and rice are brought separately to the table, but on the plate, rice is served over the beans, and *farofa* (manioc meal toasted or sautéed in butter with seasonings like salt, garlic, onion, and sometimes bacon, olives, and eggs) is sprinkled over the rice. *Farofa* may be eaten as a side dish; a more common topping for *feijoada* is *farinha* or *farinha de mandioca*, raw manioc meal served either in tall bottles or small bowls. Coffee is served after the meal. *Lanche,* a light snack or small sandwich, might be taken at midafternoon by those who are at home.

The evening meal is often light by North American standards and may be served anywhere from seven to nine o'clock. Meals are generally regarded as a social event, a time to relax and visit, particularly the noon and evening meals. Conversation during meals is generally light. Because Brazilians enjoy arguing a point, subjects like religion, politics, and other controversial matters are best left until after the meal, over coffee.

Except for breakfast, coffee is not served with a meal but after the meal, following dessert. It may be served at the table or away from the table in a living or sitting room, and it might be brewed and served in the same room or it might be brewed in the kitchen with individual cups brought in on a tray and passed around. Called *cafezinho,* Brazilian after-dinner coffee is very strong and very sweet. Darkly roasted, reminiscent of espresso coffee though not quite as potent, it is served in demitasse cups and sipped slowly. The coffee may be brewed in two ways, either by using a paper or cloth filter *(coador)* through which boiling water is poured over the grounds (sugar might be added to the ground coffee in the filter), or by boiling water, adding the coffee, boiling the water a second time and then straining it. Sugar is usually added when the coffee is poured by whoever is serving. Because the coffee is so sweet, it is generally not served with desserts, like cake or cookies. Because it is so strong, most Brazilians drink only one cup, though one certainly may drink more. A liqueur might follow the coffee, but *cafezinho* usually completes a meal. *Cafezinho* is also offered to visitors, and again, it would be served after rather than with food.

During a meal, Brazilians rarely drink milk. Instead, they often drink water, carbonated beverages (*guaraná* is very popular), fruit punches, cashew fruit juice, or *maracujá* (passion fruit). Fruit juices are particularly common at Sunday meals and at afternoon snacks. Brazilians might order soft drinks at a fine restaurant, in which case both the bottle and a glass are brought to the table, and the drink is served without ice.

Formal Brazilian table etiquette is much like formal North American table etiquette, and table manners serve as an indicator of social standing in Brazil. The degree of formality depends, of course, upon the particular situation (manners can be relaxed at home with family and close friends), but graceful and gracious eating is valued as a sign of good breeding and a sign of respect for one's companions. North Americans often do not make the best appearance at a Brazilian dinner table, largely because of the tendency to use their hands when eating, as described earlier. Another North American habit that Brazilians notice and find objectionable is that of politely excusing oneself, often while lightly tapping or patting the mouth or the chest with palm or fingertips, after an accidental belch. One common first-interview comment from Brazilians was "You Americans, you belch all the time." Of course, most North Americans do not belch all the time and also describe the habit as rude. The Brazilian response is probably because of two factors. First, they find the habit highly offensive and so its occurrence is noticed and remembered. Second, should a Brazilian belch, he or she would probably not apologize as that would only call attention to the fact, but might ignore the *faux pas*. Likewise, if one feels a sneeze or a cough coming on, he should ideally leave the table and should certainly turn around, away from the group. Brazilians do, however, make discreet use of toothpicks (*palitos*) while sitting at the table, covering the mouth with one hand or with the napkin while the toothpick is in use. Toothpicks can be found on most Brazilian tables, both in homes and in restaurants, in a small holder called a *paliteiro*. One reader reported that the *paliteiro* "sometimes replaces the expected pepper shaker. Many a North American has tried to pepper his food to find he has covered it with toothpicks."[1] Never are toothpicks displayed by the cashier's desk in a Brazilian restaurant, and to walk out of a restaurant using or chewing on a toothpick is considered extremely impolite.

Silverware is used much as in North America, though the place setting may differ (figure 8). At a formal dinner, where a place setting contains several spoons and/or forks, one begins with the outside pieces. The knife might lie alone to the right of the plate, and one might find a special knife for fish with a shorter, wider blade. The spoon(s) might lie on the left, nearest the plate, or above the plate, parallel to the edge of the table. When a meal or an individual course is finished, the utensils are placed across the plate, sometimes across the far side of the plate and pointing toward the user, though the utensils should not be overlapped. Silverware on the plate and the napkin placed beside the plate are signs one has finished eating.

During the meal, the fork is usually held constantly, and since Brazilians keep both hands above the table while eating, the knife may be held also. The North American habit of eating with one hand in the lap strikes Brazilians as very odd and may spark jokes about injuries to the hidden arm. When not being held, the knife rests with the handle on the table with the tip resting on the side of the plate. While not considered particularly polite, the knife may be used to push food onto the fork. One should always use the knife, never the edge of the fork, to cut anything (some varieties of Brazilian lettuce, by the way, are folded with knife and fork rather than cut). Pieces of meat should be cut and eaten one at a time,

Figure 8
Formal Brazilian table setting

and some Brazilians do, in formal situations, shift the fork from the left hand to the right hand to eat. Many Brazilians, however, keep the fork in the left hand rather than shift the fork from left hand to right and back again. While talking, one should rest the silverware on the plate.

Brazilians generally sit at a table to eat a meal. The table itself is covered with a cloth; place mats are considered "very American" and are usually called *jogo Americano*—"American set." Another "very American" food custom is eating buffet style. During a Brazilian meal, food is served from platters on the table. Depending upon the number of people to be served, several platters might be used so that each person helps himself from a platter without having to pass either platters or plates around the table. At a formal dinner party, men serve the women seated beside them, though the host(ess) may hire a waiter or maid to help with the serving of the meal on a special occasion.

Restaurants in Brazil range from formal restaurants that demand formal table manners to *pastelarias* (small street cafes or stands selling *pastel*, an eggroll-like dough filled with meat or cheese) and *barzinhos*, street-corner bars. The last two serve food and often alcohol, and range from small stands selling snacks to bars or cafes with tables. In Bahia, a *barzinho* is a bar for young people. *Barzinhos* are popular places for young people to meet and are found frequently on the beaches. Stores in Bahia called *vendas* or *vendinhas* have bars. In São Paulo, a bar is a more expensive, upper class establishment. *Barzinhos* are casual establishments and are found on nearly every street corner. There, a *barzinho* might sell bread and milk as well as drinks. The quality of the food varies greatly in these establishments, but the general appearance should give the prospective patron a clue as to the quality of the food and the nature of the clientele. Unescorted women do not frequent *barzinhos*, and even groups of women unfamiliar with an area should probably avoid *barzinhos* if they do not see other women present inside. *Barzinhos* are casual and behavior in them is informal.

In an average or popular restaurant, patrons seat themselves. In a formal restaurant, the *garçon* (Brazilian formal restaurants employ waiters, not waitresses) leads patrons to a table, seats the women first, and then seats the men. Once the patrons are seated in a formal restaurant, the *garçon* should be attentive and the meal should proceed much as it would in a formal North American restaurant. In a popular restaurant, however, patrons

may have to call the waiter when they want to order or if they
want something during the meal, and getting his attention might
be difficult. If a man is in the party, he calls the waiter and places
the order for the group. If a group of women are ordering, one
woman usually orders for the group.

To attract a waiter's attention, one should begin with a glance,
arching the eyebrows slightly and beckoning with the index
finger of an upraised hand. One can also use the paralinguistic
"psiu-psiu," though this would not be used in a formal restaurant.
Depending upon the establishment itself and such variables as
the number of patrons and the noise levels, a man might tug the
waiter's arm as he passed the table. A woman would not tug at a
waiter's elbow, but then female patrons are likely to receive more
attention from Brazilian waiters than are male patrons. Tapping a
glass or snapping one's fingers is considered extremely rude
(snapping the fingers, in particular, is used to call a dog or a cat),
though if other means of gaining the waiter's attention fail, these
may be used.

In a fast food or a very informal restaurant, the bill is paid
either when one orders or when the food is served. In most
restaurants, however, patrons must ask the waiter for the bill.
Brazilians find the North American habit of leaving the bill on the
table quite disturbing, "as though they want you to leave," or "as
though they think you won't pay." Figure 9 shows a common
gesture that asks for the bill. The gesture mimics the writing of a

Figure 9
"Check please!"

bill and can be performed either on one open palm held in the air or on the table top.

The waiter brings one bill that may not be itemized. The waiter does *not* bring separate bills for individuals. When the waiter brings the bill, either one person pays the entire amount, or it is split evenly among group members. Brazilians find the North American custom of separate checks odd, and the habit of figuring just who owes what on the bill very petty. If one man is with a woman or even several women, he pays the entire amount, and a Brazilian man may very well be offended if a woman insists on paying all or even part of the bill. If men are present, or if the group is all male or all female, some negotiating over the bill takes place. If the meal was the result of an invitation, particularly if the meal was fairly inexpensive, the person who extended the invitation should pay, though other group members should protest. If the meal was expensive, and/or was a casual, spontaneous gathering, the bill is usually divided evenly among group members. Brazilians find the North American concern over exact amounts and fair portions silly. A woman from Belo Horizonte was not particularly concerned about bills being evenly divided: "When you have more, you give more; when you have less, you give less. It all works out in the end." One must not take advantage of the system. The person who never protests but always lets others pay the bill, or the person who consistently orders more expensive items and then splits the bill with the group runs the risk of being labelled as stingy and will probably wind up dining alone.

Brazilians tip frequently, and one should certainly tip a waiter. Many restaurants add a service charge *(serviço)* to the bill, and a diner need not add to that. If the tip is not included in the bill, the diner should not follow the American custom of leaving money on the table. Rather, a small tip could be handed, discreetly, directly to the waiter, or one could overpay the bill by a small amount and leave before receiving change.

A word should be added about public restrooms in Brazil. Public facilities are not as common there as in the United States, particularly outside major urban centers. Restaurants frequently provide a facility for handwashing outside the restroom proper. Diners may wash their hands before being seated or may leave the table after ordering to wash their hands while the food is being prepared. One situation in which Brazilians might *not* shake hands in greeting is across the dinner table, after diners have washed. For much of Brazil, inside flushing toilets that can handle toilet paper are relatively new. In the past, paper was thrown in a basket beside the toilet; if no basket is there, paper might end up on the floor. Both Brazilians and North Americans agree that public restrooms should be avoided if possible, especially when traveling. Brazilian men, particularly truck drivers, stop by the side of the road and use the side of their truck. Although North Americans find this rather alarming and Brazilians find it "low class," it is not considered indecent. At the same time, a Brazilian woman remarked that North American public restrooms bothered her because the doors on the stalls never reach from floor to ceiling, so others can see one's feet and sometimes one's head.

A word should also be added about alcohol. Brazil has no age restrictions on buying alcohol, though a person must be eighteen to drink it. Brazilians do drink, and bars sometimes stay open all night, but Brazilians do not drink to get drunk and they are surprised by what they see as the North American overemphasis on drinking and being drunk. Being drunk shows ill breeding and lack of respect for oneself and for others and is considered low class. Women can drink in public, though not as much as men, and certainly not to the point of being drunk. Women should probably not go into bars unescorted, particularly *barzinhos*.

Beer is sometimes considered a man's drink; women tend to drink wine, liqueurs, and hard liquors. All Brazilians, even in the poorest *barzinhos*, drink from glasses, not from bottles or cans. *Cachaça, pinga,* and *aguardente* are three names for a popular liquor. It is like tequila but made from sugar cane. Men drink it straight. A very popular drink combines *pinga* with lemons and sugar to make *caipirinha*. These drinks are potent, and should be savored by slow sipping, like cognac or whiskey, which are also consumed in Brazil. A *batida* (means "beaten") is made from *pinga*, fruit, sugar, and perhaps condensed milk, put through a blender with ice. It is not as strong as some other Brazilian drinks and might be served to teenagers for a special event, like a birthday party. The precise definition of a *batida* varies from region to region, and in a few areas, a *batida* may not contain alcohol.

Some general North American attitudes toward food and eating that Brazilians find odd, or amusing, or sometimes rude include weight loss and vegetarian diets. Brazilians accept excuses for not eating, but they are not particularly sympathetic toward Americans' obsession with weight. A woman "should look like she likes her body." A diet could suggest just the opposite. When invited to a meal, particularly when the invitation comes from outside the upper or upper-middle classes, one is expected to eat and to eat a lot. Vegetarian diets are not common in Brazil, so any restrictions against eating meat should be made clear in advance.

Notes

1. John B. Jensen, Florida International University, personal communication, November 17, 1981.

EVENTS

Parties

Among young people (university students, for example), parties may be casual and spontaneous events given to mark a specific event or given just for the sake of socializing. Americans should be aware, however, that in many Brazilian circles, parties are more elaborate and more formal occasions than in the United States. Many households have a servant or servants to help with preparations, and a hostess may spend several days preparing or supervising the preparation of fancy homemade hors d'oeuvres and sweets. Such preparations, along with the general attitude toward privacy in the home, make parties in the home less common in Brazil than in the United States. Parties often take place in a private club, and some clubs hold regular parties for teenagers, setting aside specific times for specific groups with common interests. Inviting a large number of acquaintances or business associates into the home could very well be seen as a breach of privacy, particularly since a person invited to a party is free to bring along a friend or friends of his own who may be strangers to their host(ess). People living alone are much freer to give parties in their homes or apartments, but the extended family is still the dominant living pattern in Brazil, so individuals do not often live alone. Some Brazilians feel a party held in a club inplies a higher status than a party held in a home, particularly parties held for a special occasion like a wedding or a girl's fifteenth birthday and debut.

Parties involve food, drinks (generally both alcoholic and nonalcoholic), music, and particularly for young people, dancing. Dancers may perform in couples (either a man and a woman or two women) or individually, and if the crowd is large, the occasion festive, and the space ample, a number of people might form a line to dance *sambas* or *marchas*, dances associated specifically with *Carnaval*. Parties tend to be focused on partic- ular age groups or interest groups (young people, young married people, older married people, etc.) and people at a party tend to separate themselves into smaller groups. Women may congregate in the kitchen and men in the living room, or women may cluster on one side of the room and men on the other. If a party involves teenagers and adults, the teenagers form one group and the adults another. One reason given for this separation is that one group has little to say to the other—teenagers have more to say to other teenagers than to adults, and women have more in common with other women than with men. Another suggestion was that the presence of women might dampen some of male conversation, and yet another explanation, directed specifically at couples, was that close interaction between one man's wife or girlfriend and another man would lead to jealousy and perhaps to fighting.

Guests traditionally do not bring anything to a party. The host(ess) provides all food and drink. This custom is changing, particularly among younger people, as prices rise and entertaining becomes more expensive. Students might take up a collection to buy food and drink for a party, or the student host(ess) might ask guests to bring something. Still, the custom of guests contributing to the party fare is not nearly as common in Brazil as in the United States. Parties begin late by North American standards, partly because Brazilians may not eat dinner until seven or eight o'clock and partly because Brazilians arrive later than the announced time of the event. A prospective partygoer should *not* arrive at the stated time. Fifteen minutes to a half hour late is considered on time, and except for dinner parties, one can probably arrive considerably later. North Americans who are concerned with arriving precisely on time may find their host(ess) not yet ready for company. One of our first interviews involved visiting two families (one of which was Brazilian) in a nearby town with which we were unfamiliar. We lost our way finding the Brazilian home and arrived at least a half hour late, apologetic and embarrassed, only to find our host in a T-shirt taking out the trash, not the least disturbed by our "lateness." However, an invitation that specifies "American time," "Swiss time," or "British time," means guests should arrive at a designated time.

When guests arrive at a party, whether or not they are introduced depends upon the size of the gathering. If it is large, few if any introductions are made. If it is small, new arrivals may be introduced to some members of the group, and perhaps to the entire group. As described earlier, Brazilians are not as concerned with introductions as are North Americans and so do not feel obliged to introduce each guest. If introductions are made, they will probably use only the first name and any appropriate title, not the last name. Whether or not departing guests say goodbyes to the group also depends upon the size of the gathering, though a guest should certainly say goodbye to his host(ess). If the party is a small one, and if a guest knows he will leave early, he should say so when he arrives, giving a reason for his early departure. If he does not, his early departure will cause other guests to feel uneasy. "Early" and "late" are, of course, relative, but Brazilian social events often extend into the early hours of the morning. A weekend party might not begin to disperse until 2:00 A.M.

Dinner parties are also less common in Brazil than in the United States, and again, this is partly because Brazilians are not nearly so casual about inviting acquaintances or business associates into their homes as are North Americans. As stated earlier, a foreigner is much more likely to be invited to dinner at a restaurant or club than to a Brazilian home. North Americans are somewhat taken aback by this custom, as we tend to invite people into our homes for dinner almost automatically and consider an invitation to a restaurant as somewhat formal and distant, a misinterpretation from the Brazilian point of view. A second reason that dinner parties are less common in Brazil is that they are extremely elaborate events. One Brazilian described the situation thus: "When you're entertaining, do it right. People say 'It's the thought,' but they do look at the work and care involved in preparing the party. It should be a real occasion, a real event. Parties are just that much harder to give. You spend a lot. People will be offended if you don't do it right." An invitation to dinner is a gesture of hospitality and esteem; an invitation to dinner in a Brazilian home is a very special gesture of hospitality and esteem.

A guest at a formal dinner or special occasion might have flowers sent to the hostess before the meal or might bring flowers to present to the hostess when he arrives. Fresh flowers are inexpensive in Brazil, so if a guest brings flowers, he should bring a large bouquet. A guest would probably not bring a hostess a gift like a bottle of wine, though if he were to bring wine, it should be a very good one.

As with other social occasions, Brazilian dinner parties begin late in the evening, particularly if the dinner is at a club or restaurant, when it might not begin until ten or eleven o'clock.

Guests gather for hors d'oeuvres, drinks, and conversation before dinner, and this before-dinner visit may be lengthy. If the dinner is in the home, the hostess has the food ready beforehand, besides having a maid to help with last minute details. Brazilians are surprised by the North American habit of leaving guests in order to finish preparing the meal. Even the glasses intended for use should be washed, ready, and waiting. "It shows you have prepared for your guests." A Brazilian guest in the United States will probably offer to help with dinner but expects the offer to be refused. A Brazilian guest in Brazil would probably not offer to help. If an American guest offered to help a Brazilian host(ess) with dinner, the Brazilian might be amused, though if unaware of North American customs, he or she might be somewhat taken aback. "Your offer suggests they aren't doing a good job or that they can't afford a maid." Likewise, one should not bring a gift of food or offer to contribute to the meal. "You're suggesting they don't have enough." The meal is quite likely to be served by a maid or even a waiter, or several platters of food might be set on the table to remove the need for passing dishes from person to person. "American style" means buffet and is not common in Brazil.

As with social parties, these rules are relaxing among some groups. University students get together for potluck dinners, but the custom is by no means common. If a guest does bring food to a party, any leftovers should be left with the host or hostess. Even the dish containing the food should be left. "Asking for your dish," said one Brazilian woman, "is just like asking for your food." A host or hostess returning such a dish generally prepares something edible to put in it. "It's not an absolute obligation, but we usually do. It's nice."

Birthdays

A birthday or *aniversário* is a very important event in Brazil and is celebrated accordingly. Although the celebration may become less elaborate as celebrants grow older, birthdays should be acknowledged personally and are most likely celebrated with a party. Guests should bring a gift to a birthday party, though the gift need not be elaborate, particularly if you have been invited to a party for someone you do not know well. Children's birthday celebrations include a cake with candles and perhaps paper flowers (Brazilians use frosting decorations and writing less frequently than do Americans), homemade snacks and candy, soft drinks, toys and noisemakers. Family members, neighbors, and friends from school attend, and while the party is staged largely for children, adults attend as well. Mothers may compete to see who can give the best birthday party. Children's parties are not organized with specific games or activities, but instead focus on the cake. Brazilians follow the same ritual as do North Americans of singing "Happy Birthday" and blowing out the candles before cutting the cake. The following words accompany the same tune North Americans use for "Happy Birthday to You":

Parabéns p'ra você	(Congratulations to you
Nesta data querida	On this special date
Muitas felicidades	Lots of happiness
Muitos anos de vida!	And long life!)

Brazilians clap while singing and hug the birthday person afterward. Birthday spankings are *not* a custom in Brazil.

Particularly important for middle and upper class families is a girl's fifteenth birthday, her debut into society. The celebration is large and may be held in a club or rented hall. At a set time during the evening, generally at midnight, the celebrant dances a waltz with her father, then with her escort while fifteen of her close female friends or relatives dance with their escorts. The girls dress in white and sometimes hold candles.

Adult birthday parties may not include candles on the cake, but include a decorated cake and an enormous amount of food and drink. Most of the food is homemade and includes both sweets (*doces*) and salty hors d'oeuvres (*salgadinhos*), and drink includes both alcoholic and nonalcoholic beverages. The cake is not cut until late at an adult's party, and may not be cut at all. Rather, it might be saved and shared with close friends the following day. Punch and food are set out buffet-style and guests help themselves. The giving of gifts is common for adult birthdays as well as for children's. Brazilians value generosity and so give gifts frequently. Boyfriends and girlfriends exchange little gifts regularly, apart from specific occasions like birthdays, but such exchanges do not indicate a serious relationship. In addition to giving gifts more often, some Brazilians give more intimate gifts than would North Americans, ranging from shirts and T-shirts to bikinis and underwear. Such gifts do not indicate the same degree of intimacy in Brazil that they would in North America. Still, the primary focus of birthdays generally and adult birthdays specifically is celebrating with people—family, friends, and close acquaintances. "Everyone goes to everyone else's birthday. It expresses the value of the person in society." Family members may prepare a special dinner for family and close friends only, in addition to the large party, and a family member will probably take charge of organizing the larger party. The idea that a person might be alone on his birthday is unthinkable to Brazilians. If a Brazilian could not attend a friend's birthday celebration (considered highly unlikely by those we interviewed), he would stop by the friend's house with a card, telephone his regrets, or have a friend deliver the card. In keeping with the Brazilian penchant for person-to-person interaction, he would not mail the card unless the friend were in a different city or town.

Weddings

Brazilian weddings are preceded by separate parties for the bride and groom, but not by the multiple wedding showers expected by North Americans. The groom's party is much like a North American bachelor party, though it is held in a bar or club and men bring small gifts for the groom, often bar accessories. The bride's party, held in her best friend's kitchen, differs a great deal from a North American wedding shower. Friends of the bride bring small gifts, usually kitchen accessories, and play jokes on the bride. She may be dressed in odd clothes, her face might be painted, or she might be asked to guess what is in a series of packages, removing a piece of clothing when she guesses wrong. A party for both bride and groom is not unheard of, but the above celebrations are much more common.

Wedding gifts are delivered to the bride's house before the ceremony and are opened as they are received. The wedding may involve two ceremonies, a civil ceremony held in the home or registry office, required by federal law, and a church ceremony, often held on a Friday night. Weddings held during the week (Monday through Thursday) are a sign of status and are considered chic. The bride dresses nicely for the civil ceremony, and family members are present, but the church ceremony is the more public and more elaborate of the two. The practice of combining the civil service with the religious service held in a church is becoming increasingly common. It is a formal event, beginning with a church service (usually a Nuptial Mass since Brazil is predominantly Catholic) and ending with a large party for friends and family, held sometimes in the bride's home but more often in a private club or rented hall. Drinks, sweets, and hors d'oeuvres are served. Brazilians serve wedding cake but not groom's cake. Wedding anniversaries are celebrated with small family parties, though the twenty-fifth, the fiftieth, and the seventy-fifth are special events and are celebrated accordingly.

Funerals

Large towns in Brazil have funeral homes, just as in North America, but in smaller towns and rural areas, the body might be displayed at a church, in a hospital, or in the home. The custom of embalming is not common in Brazil. Consequently, funerals take place within twenty-four hours of a death (often on the same day if a death occurs in the morning), and the entire period is given over to public expressions of grief and condolence. A wreath of purple flowers on a door indicates a *velório* (watch or wake) in progress inside.

During the *velório*, the night before the funeral, family members and close friends sit with the body, and friends, acquaintances, and business associates come to offer sympathy, stay a while, and depart. Mourners express their grief openly through words and tears, regardless of sex or age. Conversation during a *velório* includes discussion of the deceased, his personal qualities and events in his life, and women may tell traditional stories not specifically related to the deceased. Mourners may partake of coffee, food, and sometimes alcohol throughout the *velório*. In the past, women wore black at funerals and a wife wore black for a year following her husband's death, but dark colors are now acceptable in place of black. One gradually fading custom is the wearing, by family members, of a small strip of black fabric, or two crossed strips of black fabric over the heart. The piece of fabric is worn the day of the funeral and at subsequent Masses for the deceased, held seven days, thirty days, and one year after the funeral. Many people attend the funeral and the seven-day Mass, but later Masses are generally attended only by family and very close friends. In some areas of Brazil, women may not accompany the body to the cemetery. After the burial, only the closest family members return home with the bereaved. Brazilians are shocked by the North American custom of funeral guests returning to a relative's home for a meal with the family. After a funeral, the family of the deceased sends cards to friends and acquaintances announcing the death. The cards, sent to those who attended the funeral as well as to those who did not, often carry a picture of the deceased. Sometimes a family pays for a radio announcement of the death, and such an announcement might contain a lengthy list of family members participating in the announcement. On November first, All Souls' Day, relatives visit family graves to pray and to decorate the gravesites with flowers and sometimes with lighted candles.

Holidays and Festivals

Brazilian national holidays include Flag Day (November 19) and Discovery Day (April 22) which are celebrated in schools and by local military groups, but not by the general public. Independence Day (September 7) is marked by a week-long celebration beginning August 31 with bands, parades, special sports events, and gymnastic exhibitions. Labor Day (May 1) is celebrated only by *operários*—blue collar workers and laborers. Unions organize barbeques and sports events, and large factories might organize special events for factory workers. Business and government offices are closed for the holidays, though restaurants and movie theaters usually remain open.

Popular holidays include *Dia dos Namorados* (June 12), the Brazilian equivalent of Valentine's Day, and three religious-popular festivals in June dedicated to Saint Anthony (June 13), Saint John (June 24), and Saint Peter (June 29). Unmarried women celebrate Saint Anthony's day with a special mass, after which they donate thirteen centavos to the Saint in hopes he will find them a husband. These Saints' Days are celebrated with bonfires, balloons, fireworks, and costumes. Celebrants wear patched clothes and rural dress. Parties may include a mock sheriff and a mock jail, as well as a bride and groom, whose marriage is followed by a dance similar to the North American square dance, called the *quadrilha*. These activities commemorate Brazil's rural heritage. Special drinks include *caipirinha*, *pinga* with lemon and sugar, or a drink of *pinga* with clove and cinnamon, and in São Paulo, hot wine drinks called *quentão* or *vinho quente*. Special foods include corncakes, sweet potatoes, peanuts, popcorn, hominy cooked with nuts, and peanut flour eaten by itself or with cooked banana. In São Paulo, *canjica* is a sweet-tasting corn soup, but in most of Brazil (especially the Northeast) it is a traditional candy associated with these Saints' Days made with corn, coconut, sugar, milk, and cinnamon. In Bahia, celebrants might go from house to house visiting and eating, whether or not they know the residents.

Children's Day, *Cosme e Damião*, resembles Americans' Halloween. Parents and relatives give gifts and candy to children on the streets and in buses, and poor children may line up outside houses or, more commonly, outside certain institutions or stations to receive small bags of candy. Adults should give candy to the children of friends and acquaintances.

By far the largest and best known of Brazilian popular holidays is *Carnaval*, a four-day celebration with dancing, drinking, costumes, and parades, ending on Ash Wednesday. Many businesses close, and schools are closed for summer vacation, so Brazilians can dedicate the entire period to celebration. One Brazilian woman observed, "In *Carnaval* you can almost change your personality; it's like another self comes out of you." In the words of another, "It's like a parade, but it's a mess!" Celebrations take place in homes and at private clubs, but the bulk of the celebrating happens at night and in the streets, profusely decorated for the occasion. A traditional feature of *Carnaval* is the competition between various Samba schools (groups or clubs). The Samba schools began in the nineteenth century in different Black communities and for decades served as a primary means of expression for oppressed Blacks. The *Carnaval* competitions, however, have become popularized and very commercial, attracting large numbers of wealthy outsiders. The foreigner should be careful during *Carnaval*, for as is true of any large public event, many pickpockets are plying their own trade amongst the revelers. Any celebration anywhere at any time of year can take on the characteristics of *Carnaval*. Said one North American, "Brazilians can make *carnaval* anywhere. They just need *carnaval* music and room to dance."

Religious holidays include Easter, celebrated with a half-week holiday and the giving of chocolate bunnies and eggs to children, and Good Friday, recognized with a meatless dinner. Young men sometimes mark the Saturday after Good Friday by hanging or burning an effigy of Judas.

Christmas is primarily a family holiday, though employer/ employee celebrations are not uncommon if the relationship is a close one, and Brazilians do send Christmas cards to close friends and acquaintances. On Christmas day, close friends might visit one another's families to share a drink or a sweet snack, but most of the celebrating takes place within the home and within the family.

A traditional Christmas would begin with midnight Mass on Christmas eve, called *Missa do Galo* (literally, the Rooster's Mass). A more conservative family might include family prayers upon returning home from Mass. After Mass, family members gather to visit, perhaps exchange gifts with more distant relatives (Brazilians, like North Americans, settle the question of who buys for whom amongst more distant relatives by the drawing of names), and enjoy an informal meal of cold turkey and other buffet-type foods. Gifts are generally kept under a tree, and in the past, the Brazilian Christmas tree has been an evergreen tree decorated like its North American counterpart. Recently, though, Brazilians have begun to use trees native to Brazil, so in areas like Bahia one might find a branch of a native tree rather than a non-native evergreen. The lunch served on Christmas day might indicate the same desire to follow Brazilian rather than European or American patterns, as some Brazilians are beginning to replace traditional turkey, *presunto tender* (ham), or *leitoa assada* (roasted suckling pig) with fruit, vegetable salads, and lighter, summer fare.

Family celebrations play an important role in New Year's celebrations also, but New Year's is a far more public holiday than is Christmas. A family might begin the celebration with a midnight Mass, and Mass might be followed by a large family meal or by a family gathering with drinks and light snacks. During both Christmas and New Year's, the family table should always be set, even if the family is not at home, so that all will be ready should visitors arrive. The major New Year's celebration, called *Reveillon*, takes place after the family celebration and generally in a club, though rising costs are resulting in more at-home *Reveillon* celebrations. *Reveillon* "turns into *Carnaval*." Celebrants wear special clothes, though not necessarily costumes, dance Samba in clubs and in the streets, and generally give themselves over to the celebration. Most people dance until sunrise, as watching the sun rise is a customary part of the event, and many continue through New Year's Day without sleep. "It's like *Carnaval*, only one day instead of four." The Festival of Iemanjá, the goddess/queen of the sea, marks New Year's celebrations in coastal areas. Thousands of people gather on the beaches to launch small boats filled with offerings or to throw flowers as an offering into the sea. *Macumba* ceremonies involving dances, prayer, and trances may also be a part of the festival.

Audience Behavior

Theaters and Movie Theaters

"Theater" in Brazil, as in much of the United States, means a play and a fairly formal occasion. Tickets are more expensive and playgoers dress well. Candy might be sold in the theater lobby or perhaps by young boys outside the entrance, but generally audience members do not eat during a performance. Audience members might clap during the play for a particularly outstanding scene, but applause is generally reserved for the end of the performance.

Again like the United States, movies are much more casual than the theater, though evening movies (which may start at eight o'clock or as late as ten) are more formal than afternoon movies regarding both dress and behavior. Moviegoers may form lines, and if so, late arrivers try to crowd in ahead and those already in line protest loudly. If the crowd does not form a line, individuals push a path to the outside ticket window and push a path to the lobby door. Lobbies are often small and, by North American standards, crowded. "People are smoking. Guys kiss their girlfriends. Everyone pushes and shoves, but people just laugh, don't get angry about it." Brazilians eat during a movie, but only candy or a small bag of popcorn. Brazilians are surprised by the North American custom of serving soft drinks in movie theaters and by the size of the drink cups and popcorn containers. Another North American custom that Brazilians find amusing is that of occasionally clapping during or after a movie, "when there's no one there to hear it." While conversations do take place during movies, they should be kept low.

Americans will probably notice a relatively high noise level during a Brazilian movie, as Brazilians, especially young men, comment loudly on and perhaps joke about the movie. This audible commentary is considered rude by Brazilians, but it does happen, particularly at afternoon movies with a younger audience. One explanation for such conversation is that only recently have Brazilians begun making films. Previously, all films were foreign and were subtitled. Further, theaters often had very poor sound systems—not a problem if the audience reads subtitles rather than listens to the sound.[1]

Movies and movie theaters provide a common context for a Brazilian adolescent's first unsupervised interaction with the opposite sex, and this flirtatious interaction can become fairly rowdy. Teenage girls, who often do most of the flirting, sit together but try to sit in front of or behind the fellows they want to attract. They giggle, talk, and sometimes throw paper to get the fellows' attention, though often when those fellows begin a conversation, the girls coyly turn away. A teenage boy might ask a girl for her phone number, and if she is interested in pursuing the acquaintance, she gives it to him.

Older men might comment on women at a movie as they do on the streets, and some men might attempt to touch a woman in a crowded theater. This is definitely considered rude by Brazilian women, but it does happen. The North American might want to check with Brazilian acquaintances or a tourist information center if he is unsure about a particular theater. Some smaller theaters outside the downtown areas of larger cities are frequented by less-than-savory representatives of Brazilian social life.

Sports Events

Soccer (called *futebol* in Brazil) is by far the most popular public sport in Brazil. Tennis is common among the upper and upper-middle classes, as are horse racing and golf; boxing is becoming more popular in some cities, and basketball enjoys a limited audience, but most Brazilians are soccer fans. Good soccer players are greatly admired and soccer rivalries can terminate friendships. The government funds many social services through the proceeds from a weekly sports lottery based exclusively on soccer games.

Sports are based on clubs rather than universities or cities. Every city has a club, and some cities have several, many of which originated in the last century as social organizations for immigrants. When soccer became popular, the clubs used members' dues to support a team. At a game, members try to dress in club colors and carry flags and hats bearing the club colors and mascot. Seating sections in stadiums are separated by clubs, and members should sit in the appropriate section. Emotions run high during Brazilian soccer games, and sitting in the wrong section could lead to harassment and possibly fighting.

One can attend a game and sit apart from the clubs. The general seating is divided into three tiers, with the most expensive being the bottom tier close to the field. Most people sit in the middle area. The third or upper tier has the cheapest seats, and it is by far the rowdiest section of the stadium, one which women should probably avoid. One might see fights in these sections, and people throw things. Brazilian clubs do not use cheerleaders, but crowd members sing songs to spur the game. Some of these songs are parodies of popular songs and many of them are obscene. When a goal is scored, people jump up and down, throw hats, shirts, and flags into the air, and hug one another. In the words of a Brazilian enthusiast, "They just go crazy!" Because behavior can be quite rowdy, people entering the stadium are often frisked for alcohol, guns, and knives. Alcohol is not allowed in the seating area, but it is sold from a bar in the stadium, where police make sure no one takes it out of the bar.

After a game, clubs celebrate a victory in the streets, and sometimes these celebrations become small carnavals with celebrants dancing, shouting, drinking, and driving through the streets with car horns blaring. When a club finally won the city championship for São Paulo in 1977 after trying for twenty-three years, the celebrations lasted three days. "Generally the defeated club accepts its status quietly, though when Brazil was disqualified from the World Soccer Cup in 1966, one São Paulo office building marked the loss by throwing black typewriter ribbons from office windows."

Notes

1. John B. Jensen, Florida International University, personal communication, November 17, 1981. Readers interested in a detailed study of Brazilian movies and the Brazilian movie industry may wish to consult Randal Johnson's *Brazilian Cinema* (forthcoming).

BEHAVIOR in PUBLIC

Dress

Brazilians possess a strong sense of personal presentation in public. Almost any appearance in public provides an opportunity to observe and be observed; hence careful and fashionable dress assumes a great importance as an indication of status, of self-respect, and of respect for others. Poor or incorrect dress could offend a host, indicating a lack of sufficient respect and concern for the other to dress appropriately. A Brazilian woman described the Brazilian attitude toward dress as "highly critical. If you don't have the right clothes, you stay home." As the section on street etiquette suggests, Brazilians have a strong sense of display, a sense that one should display oneself to the best advantage. Brazilian women in particular possess an ingrained confidence that to be a woman is to be looked at and admired. A Brazilian man might be stopped by the police if he drives without wearing a shirt. This sense of display often results in a strong sense of personal presence and a concern for dress and personal appearance that contrasts sharply at times with the gererally casual North American approach to dress. A Brazilian man commented that upper and middle class Brazilians dress up more than do North Americans. He had never seen people wearing blue jeans with patches or holes before coming to the United States, and he assumed at first that such dress was a sign of poverty. Younger people in Brazil do wear blue jeans, but they are usually tightly fitted, clean, pressed, without patches and certainly without holes.

Extremely fashion conscious, Brazilians look to Europe for models, and styles tend to follow French and Italian trends, which means tighter cuts than most Americans are accustomed to wearing. Fashions in Brazil, especially women's fashions, change every year, and everyone who can afford to change changes with them, so the outdated is immediately noticed. As noted in the discussion on business dress, one Brazilian suggested that North Americans who plan to do business or to spend much time in Brazil should plan on revising their wardrobes.

Americans are not described as good dressers by Brazilians. In fact, the jocular Brazilian stereotype of the North American tourist includes bright, loud colors that do not match, baggy clothes that do not fit, plaid pants that are too short, and the ubiquitous polyester. Added to this is the fact that most North American dress is, by Brazilian standards, at least three years behind the times. On the positive side, Brazilians confess that keeping up with fashion trends can be very expensive and that the casual American approach to dress allows one to consider comfort over style.

Upper and middle class Brazilians prefer natural fabrics, especially cottons and silks, to synthetics, in part because they have maids to help care for clothes and in part because the warm climate makes the natural fabrics much more comfortable. Comparatively heavy polyester doubleknits stand out as "very American" in Brazil. Large patterns, especially plaids and stripes, also strike Brazilians as typically American. Women might wear a plaid skirt, less often a plaid dress, but the pattern would probably be small and would be worn with solids; one would never mix patterns. A patterned skirt demands a solid blouse. Men avoid patterns in general and particularly avoid patterned pants. North Americans also tend to combine colors that a Brazilian would not, though establishing particular rules for combining colors proved difficult, and Brazilian color schemes are highly changeable because of changing styles. Brazilian men tend to wear quieter, more discreet colors than North American men, beiges and light grays or blues in warmer climates, and darker slacks (browns, grays, or black) generally. Men do not often wear blue jeans. Colors, both for men and women, tend to be earth tones and natural hues chosen to blend rather than to contrast. One color combination that is guaranteed to provoke laughter is green and yellow, used in the Brazilian flag.

As tightly fitted clothes suggest, showing off the body is part of the Brazilian sense of public appearance and public display. Another aspect of this display is the extent of exposure deemed appropriate by Brazilians for women and for men, a subject that sometimes startles and often confuses North Americans, and one that can lead to uncomfortable and sometimes disastrous situations. Most North Americans returning from Brazil remember Brazilian bathing suits which, as discussed later, are very small and very tight for both men and women. One Brazilian woman noted that "at a club or on the beach people are almost naked. That's the place for that."At the same time, women generally do not wear shorts, except in a beach town, and then only in the most casual situations, never in a business district or shopping area. Women's necklines tend to be lower and more revealing, particularly when comparing formal dress. A Brazilian man, too, reveals more of his body than does the average North American man in a similar situation. Men's clothes, like women's, tend to be more tightly fitted in Brazil. Besides being tighter, men's sport shirts worn in informal situations may be left with several buttons, sometimes all but one or two, open to reveal the chest. Brazilians describe themselves as "dressing to attract, to tease," but this teasing is one part of the broader issue of displaying one's self or presenting one's self as an attractive person, and must not be construed as a direct signal of intention or availability. It may, of course, be just such a signal, but chances are great that it is not. Brazilian dress may intend to attract, but does not necessarily intend to seduce.

Cosmetics

Brazilian women enjoy cosmetics. They use makeup frequently and, by North American standards, heavily. Most women wear makeup in public. Business and professional women almost always use makeup, and a woman dressing for a special occasion or an evening out will probably wear heavy makeup. Frequently used facial cosmetics include eyeliner, eyeshadow, blushers and rouges, and lipstick. Makeup is generally more subdued for morning and afternoon, using muted colors and earth tones, described by both North Americans and Brazilians as "the natural look." Brazilian women looking at North American fashion magazines described most of the faces as "natural, fine for daytime." The makeup worn by almost all the North American models, including those dressed for evening, was described as insufficient for an evening in Brazil. Evening makeup, besides being more heavily applied, uses brighter and more dramatic colors for eye shadows (blues, green, and purples) and darker lipsticks and rouges than the natural colors worn during the day. Colors would probably be coordinated to the clothes as well as to skin tone and hair color. Despite the penchant for heavier use of cosmetics, Brazilian women comment unfavorably on the way many North American women apply color to their cheeks with blushers or rouges, leaving a noticeable line of color along the cheek bone. The general rule seems to be that bright colors and clear contrasts are reserved for lips and eyes, while color on the cheeks should be more subtle. Many women also pluck their eyebrows to a fairly fine line, though not pencil thin by any means. Body hair is generally considered masculine, so women shave underarms and shave or wax legs.

Accessories

Rarely do Brazilians wear hats, though a woman might wear a hat for a very dressy or formal occasion, and sun visors are, as of this writing, a current fad on the beach. After the European manner, men carry large wallets which are clutched in the hand and which carry the personal documents and items that North American men would carry in a pants pocket. Men's pants are generally too tight to allow carrying anything in the pockets, and bulging pockets are a sure sign of a North American. Male students might use large shoulder bags called *bolsas para homem* to carry books and documents. Men and women wear jewelry, often gold, rarely plastic or any synthetic material. Men wear chains, sometimes heavy chains with a cross or a medallion, rings, and I.D. bracelets. Women wear a lot of jewelry—multiple chains, bracelets, rings, and earrings. Many women's ears are pierced at birth, and in the last few years, women have begun to pierce their ears more than once. Young men will occasionally pierce one ear and wear a small hoop or single stone, but this might mark the wearer as a *carioca*, a person from Rio. Women will wear perfume and most men wear colognes.

Hands and Feet

Brazilians, both men and women, take great care of their hands and feet. Women usually use nail polish, and men will trim and buff their nails. Women's nails tend to be long, and almost all women will have weekly manicures and monthly pedicures, when calluses are trimmed and nails trimmed and polished. Men usually care for their nails personally, though a man might have a manicure as a luxury. Attractive hands and feet are a sign of status and a sign that one cares about oneself, so Brazilians will notice callused feet and rough hands unfavorably.

One reason behind the concern for foot grooming is the style of shoe worn in Brazil. North American shoes seem large and somewhat clumsy to Brazilians, who wear more delicate shoes with thinner soles and more exposure of the foot. Women's shoes will often have a thin, high heel. Sandals are very common in warmer climates for both women and men. Brazilians do not often go barefoot, so sandals are the general rule on the beach. Part of the Brazilian stereotype of the American tourist is tennis shoes and white socks on the beach. Brazilian men do wear white socks with tennis shoes (the only time they will wear white socks) but never socks with sandals. Shoes and purses are generally leather, and a woman's purse should match her shoes. One North American woman "learned never to leave the house if my shoes didn't match my purse." Shoes, too, are associated with status. Good shoes in good condition and well polished (especially the highly visible toe) reflects well on the wearer. Shoes in poor condition or poorly shined reflect low status, a lack of self esteem, or both. American men's shoes sometimes look rather scruffy by Brazilian standards.

Street Etiquette

Americans, particularly women, find Brazilian street behavior highly disconcerting. One American woman, who lived in Brazil for two years working for an export firm, reported that the most difficult part of her job was walking down a public street alone. Brazilian men are, by American standards, extremely aggressive toward women on the street. To say that Brazilian men are girlwatchers is an understatement. Men will stare at a woman, sometimes staring at her face or at a particular portion of her body, sometimes giving a slow, steady, head-to-toe survey, and sometimes turning around in their tracks to stare. The stares might be accompanied by a quick, sharp "psst!" as the man passes the woman and raises his eyes to her face. Men will also comment loudly on women—loudly enough that the woman is sure to hear—and these comments range from complimentary or humorous to rude and obscene. Most Brazilians reported that such comments come primarily from lower class men or from young men who comment as much for the benefit of their peers as for the benefit of the woman, and that women have nothing to fear from this sort of exchange, but American women find this explanation of little consolation. Men might touch or pinch a woman, especially in crowded places or tight situations like a crowded bus or an elevator, but such touching is considered extremely rude. Groups of women, especially groups of young women, might stare at and offer comments about passing men, but a woman alone would never do so, unless she were either joking or trying to initiate an exchange. (Brazilian men, however, generally do not appreciate a woman taking an obvious intiative in a flirtation.) Unless a woman is accompanied by a man, she should expect this sort of attention. Groups of women and especially women alone will receive stares and comments from male passers-by.

All women must learn to cope with this sort of exchange in Brazil. Responses from Brazilian women to this behavior vary, in part because of the wide range of behaviors one might encounter, but all agreed that actual touching, obscene remarks, or crudely pointed stares are rude and insulting and should be ignored. A response, especially a smile, might be interpreted as approval or encouragement. Normally a Brazilian woman will ignore the stares and comments, or perhaps shake her head. At the same time, Brazilian women feel that North American men ignore women and that the admiring stares and complimentary remarks "make you feel like a woman." A woman might smile in response to a complimentary remark or she might laugh, but unless she wants to initiate an exchange, she must reserve any direct response until the man is out of sight or leaving. One Brazilian woman observed that men sometimes offer jokes, "and if they're funny, I'll laugh." North American women have difficulty taking this kind of behavior in stride, and one dealt with it by "staring at my feet whenever I was out alone in public." Whether they find the behavior amusing, complimentary, or insulting (and most find it a combination of the three), Brazilian women take it for granted in the anonymity of a public street.

Despite this sometimes disturbing attention to women, Brazilian men show great courtesy in matters like opening doors for women, giving them precedence when entering a doorway, and helping women with coats. As described in the Overview, the North American woman should expect and accept this, unless she wants to present the Brazilian image of a typical, pushy, North American woman. Brazilian men see such courtesies as a way of showing respect and concern, and do not understand the feeling that such attentions are demeaning. The same men who stare and comment will open a door for a woman, pick up a package she has dropped, or help her with a car door, and most Brazilian women expect and enjoy the attention.

Beaches

Most North Americans in Brazil spend at least some time on one of the many beaches, quite likely in Rio, and the first thing most will notice about public behavior on the beach is Brazilian beach dress. Men's and women's swim suits are very tight and very small to the North American eye. Men wear bikini style trunks, never the basketball shorts worn so often by North Americans. Young women wear tiny bikinis; older women and some married women may wear one piece suits, but even these are more revealing than the North American counterpart. Nearly everyone on the beach wears a swimsuit, regardless of figure, and a woman might spend hours finding a suit that shows her own shape to its best advantage. One should absolutely not, however, go into town from the beach wearing a bathing suit or even a bathing suit and coverup. Bathing suits belong on the beach or at the pool, not on the street or in a restaurant. In a resort area like Rio, women can wear shorts in casual public situations (a grocery store or a fast food restaurant), but in most parts of Brazil, shorts would be considered inappropriate public dress and a bathing suit still less appropriate. Even in Rio, one would not wear shorts downtown or to a nicer restaurant.

Brazilian beaches are places to socialize, particularly along the sidewalk area running parallel to the water between the beach proper and the town. In Rio, streets open on to the beach, so areas of the beach are identified by the names of the street leading to them, and particular groups of people (age groups or interest groups) congregate in specific areas. Boys and young men sell goods like hats, tanning oil, and bathing suit coverups, as well as food, such as fruit juices, ice cream, hot dogs, and ears of roasted corn. Food is sold from booths on the sidewalk and by young men or boys who walk along the beach with trays and who, besides crying their wares, sing and shout the time to advertise their presence. Drinks are served in cups or bottles, and sandwiches and ice cream are served wrapped in napkins, which are folded back as the item of food is eaten. Contrary to North American instinct, however, when done eating most Brazilians throw the napkin, cup, or bottle down on the beach. "There are garbage cans, but they're always full," explained one Brazilian. The government hires people to clean the beaches periodically, but North Americans will probably find the beaches considerably more littered than they might expect.

Brazilians who live near enough to the beach to go regularly generally go to the same section of beach, and so may be interacting with friends, acquaintances, or at least with people whose faces are familiar. Men and women walk along the beaches, watching and being watched. One custom that might catch an American unaware is the Brazilian practice of asking others on the beach to rub suntan lotion on one's back. Such a request is not necessarily flirtatious, though it may lead to conversation, but is regarded as a small service to another sunbather. Much flirting does take place on the beach, and because it is a place for socializing, one is free to talk with strangers. A man may try to start a conversation if he is interested in a woman, and if she is interested, she may respond. Most women would not initiate a conversation themselves, though a woman might let her gaze show her interest in a man. Much flirting is accomplished through eye contact, though men might also comment on the women they watch, often to attract a woman's attention and to begin a conversation. The comments generally address a specific part of the body, "Nice legs!" for example, and while some might be obscene, many are considered complimentary by Brazilian women and an acceptable way of expressing interest. Brazilian men generally do not start a conversation with "Hi" or "Hello," as North Americans do. Men might also bid for a women's attention with a stare, a smile, or a wink, perhaps accompanied by "psst!," or he might grab the woman's elbow, touch her shoulder, or her chin. The standard female response to this is to pull away, even if she is interested, lest she appear overanxious. If she is not interested, she might pull away quickly, making a single quick "tsk" sound while tossing her head.

Women who are obviously accompanied by men will probably not be approached at all, but most Brazilians expect this range of interaction on the beach, their attitude being that if one is interested, one may stop and talk, "and then you've made a new friend."

Paquerar is a verb meaning "to flirt." As a noun (*uma paquera*) it describes the process, the place where it occurs, or the person one flirted with. Flirting takes place on the streets, in cars, and in parks, and some streets in São Paulo are known as areas for young people to *paquerar*, to "cruise." "There's a lot of pageantry involved," explained one Brazilian, who went on to tell of a friend of his who, while riding his motorcycle, saw an attractive woman in a car going in the opposite direction. He turned his motorcycle around in the street and followed the woman. "That's nice!" commented the Brazilian women present during the conversation. Women in Brazil must be prepared for dramatic attentions from men; whether or not that attention is complimentary or insulting depends, from the Brazilian point of view, on the person, his approach, and what he says or does. An American woman should not automatically be insulted, though she will probably continue to be uncomfortable with it. Brazilians consider *paquera* as a way to meet people and may exchange phone numbers to pursue a friendship begun casually at the beach or on a street. Brazilians do not understand the American need for an introduction either through friends or through a neutral situation, like a job. "Americans need a reason to be friends," observed a woman from Belo Horizonte.

While groups of women may go out in public freely, women do not often go out in public alone. An unaccompanied woman might be assumed to be more vulnerable and must certainly expect to be approached by men. Men seeing a woman alone in a bar or at a movie might be surprised and perhaps a bit intimidated because the sight is an unusual one, but most likely they will assume she is available and looking for a man.

Public Markets

Supermarkets and department stores are common in Brazil, but they have not replaced the public markets through which farmers and other vendors can sell their products directly to consumers. Traditionally, these markets (*feiras*) moved daily around a city, and many still do, but now one might also find a single large building (*mercado*) from which vendors sell their goods. One can buy foodstuffs, like fresh produce, meats, fish and bread which is baked at the market and purchased daily by many Brazilians. Larger markets may sell clothing and other nonfood items. In cities like São Paulo, one finds *feirantes*, vendors who are middlemen, buying in bulk from farmers to sell at retail to customers. These vendors are licensed and prices are set by the government.

Market-goers may bring baskets in which to carry their purchases, and buyers are free to pick up and examine the merchandise and to select their own items. Customers generally do not form lines, and if the market is crowded (Saturday and Sunday mornings between eight and ten are the busiest times at the market), buyers simply push to the front of the booth. Hallways in a *mercado* can become quite crowded with customers, vendors, and men carrying bundles of goods to vendors, and buyers must simply push through the crowd. One need not apologize for bumping other people or things. A North American told of knocking some apples off a cart, whereupon she apologized profusely, much to the amusement of the Brazilians around her. "Americans are always apologizing for bumping people, and even for passing too close!" Most Brazilians attend the same market for years, and many patronize the same merchants, so marketing is to a certain extent a social activity. One might converse casually with strangers, particularly to ask about specific merchandise. One does not find the sort of interaction between men and women that is found on the streets or on the beach. Young boys, age thirteen or so, cluster around the entrances and offer, sometimes fairly insistently, to perform small services like carrying groceries, in return for a small tip. A firm refusal is necessary if their services are not desired.

Prices at the public markets are set by the vendors, but a certain amount of bargaining is permissible. In fact, the Brazilian government has in the recent past encouraged people to bargain as a means of fighting inflation. Not all Brazilians bargain. Some feel bargaining suggests an inability or an unwillingness to pay and others feel that the vendors need the money. Though some Brazilians might bargain in a specialty shop where they are dealing directly with the owner, the most common place for bargaining is the *feira*. "They are designed for it." When bargaining, the customer should have some idea of the item's value. If he offers too low a price, he indicates he is not serious about buying and might even offend the vendor. Brazilian bargaining is typically indirect. That is, the buyer generally does not offer a price. To do so risks "putting the seller in a bad situation, making him uncomfortable." Rather, the buyer might strike his chest with a closed fist, as though stabbing himself, while exclaiming, "Too expensive!" or *"Que facada!"* (literally, "What a stab!"). Any negotiating with the seller would be done jokingly and pleasantly, though excitedly. A man might bargain with set figures, but "That's risky and probably won't get you anywhere." A seller might offer a lower price per item for a larger quantity. Generally buyers patronize the same vendors over a period of time, so as a vendor becomes acquainted with his buyers, "he will set special things aside, what he knows you like. He might give you a discount or give you extra." If a seller gives a direct "No," then he most likely will not bargain. Further, the buyer hoping to bargain successfully should dress and act the part. "Talk to the seller in his language. Act friendly. Don't wear an expensive dress, expensive sandals." In some tourist-oriented markets, like the Salvador *Mercado Modelo*, buyers are expected to bargain as bargaining is considered part of the tourist experience.

As with most other public places in Brazil, public markets are places to watch and be watched, so careful attention to dress is advisable. Worn-out blue jeans or baggy T-shirts will probably not create a favorable impression, especially in a small town where the weekly *feira* is a social event.

Public Transportation

Larger cities in Brazil have bus systems that are efficient but very crowded. Persons waiting to board must signal the bus to stop by waving with the hand open and palm facing the bus or with the palm inverted, waist level or lower, and arm out-stretched, as though pointing to the other side of the road. Sometimes, when a bus is full, a driver will not stop, but will drive by, giving the gesture meaning "full of people" (figure 61). Older people and pregnant women are generally given consideration and allowed to board first, but most passengers have to push their way onto the bus, which is boarded at the rear and deboarded from the front. Passengers give their fares to a man in the rear of the bus, called *trocador* in Rio, *cobrador* in São Paulo, and then move through a turnstile. Fare-takers often run out of change (and many say they are out of change in any case), and fares are rarely round numbers. Riders might have to insist for the return of their change, and *cobradores* can be fairly rude in refusing. Children sometimes ride free and sometimes do not, and in either case, this may spark an argument between *cobrador* and passengers. In addition, the process of boarding and finding a seat may involve much pushing and shoving, so passengers are hardly in a position to negotiate. Some passengers always allow the *cobrador* to keep the change because he earns so little.

Once through the turnstile, most Brazilians, like most North Americans, look first for a seat alone, but passengers are generally fortunate to find a seat at all. Again, older people and pregnant women are usually offered seats, but men do not necessarily offer their seats to a woman. A seated passenger might offer to hold a child on his lap if he does not offer his seat to a woman with a child, or a passenger might offer to hold a student's books. A standing passenger might ask a seated passenger to hold a package, though women generally would not ask men. "They are so explosive in Brazil." Passengers look around at other riders "at their clothes, their books, to see what school they attend," and often strike up conversations with strangers. Brazilians enjoy conversation. "On a bus, people you don't know will start talking, telling you about themselves, asking questions about you. In a doctor's waiting room, people will talk." At the same time, crowded buses can be unpleasant. Passengers are often sitting and standing very close to one another, perhaps pressing against one another. Fights do break out on occasion, and passengers should keep their money hidden. Most men do not stare or comment on a bus as they might at a woman passing on the street, but some do and some take advantage of the crowded buses to touch or press against a woman or girl. Depending upon the severity of the action, a woman might ignore it, might shout, or might carry a hatpin and use it. For those who can afford a higher fare and who want to avoid the more crowded buses, special buses called *frescões* are available. These are more expensive, are air conditioned, and do not make as many stops. Taxis, too, are available in cities.

Tipping

One aspect of Brazilian public life that catches North Americans unaware is the custom of frequent tipping. Of course,

Brazilians tip in many of the same situations that North Americans do: waiters in restaurants, bell boys in hotels, porters in airports, taxi drivers, hairdressers, and barbers all receive tips. Brazilians also tip in some situations that a North American would not. A gas station attendant should be given a small tip, especially if he cleans the windshield, adds water to the radiator, or does anything beyond pump gas. In the cities, one encounters countless young boys who will perform small jobs for a tip. They will offer to wash windshields while cars are stopped at stop signs; they will offer to watch your car while you go into a grocery store (and, in fact, might do some minor damage if you refuse); they might, as described earlier, offer to carry your groceries to your car or perhaps carry your basket home from the *feira*, the open market; they might shine shoes, or sell papers, candy, or popcorn. The government discourages begging, but poverty is a very real problem in Brazil and a very visible problem in the cities. The general attitude toward these young boys is that they are doing what work they can, and that they need the money, so a person should offer a small tip to them.

In some cases, tips are best described as small gifts expressing appreciation rather than as gratuities given to acknowledge service. Such a case is the hospital nurse who is, as a Brazilian pointed out, the most important figure in determining how comfortable one's stay will be. The size of the tip/gift would depend upon the length of one's stay, and one would not hand the money directly to the nurse but would tuck it in an envelope or deliver it discreetly. A houseguest should remember all the housemaids with a small gift of cash when the visit ends.

Small gifts express appreciation for people one sees regularly. Maids, for instance, often receive birthday and Christmas gifts from employers. One woman told of her mother's custom of giving small Christmas gifts to the cashier and grocery boy she deals with regularly at her grocery store. Such tips and small gifts serve as a token of appreciation for a job well done. They also help foster the comfortable relationship between parties so important in Brazilian life.

A rather different use of tips also common in Brazil is the offering of tips before a service is performed, to get a job done quickly. Services might have two prices, one for quick results and the other not, or tips might be offered as gifts—a box of candy, perhaps—rather than as cash. 'The expression, 'Can you find a way to help me?' really asks 'How much?'" Two services in particular that can be complicated and time consuming are obtaining a passport and obtaining a driver's license, and Brazilians use tips to speed the process. "To get a job done faster, offer more than the set price." This use of tips is an interesting reflection of the Brazilian emphasis on the person rather than on the job or the bureaucratic machinery, just the opposite of the North American emphasis on the job or bureaucaracy rather than the person. North Americans call the Brazilian behavior "bribery" and generally feel that one should not have to offer a bribe to get a job done efficiently. According to the North American system, the mechanism should function equally well for all, regardless of the operator. Brazilians, while they may complain about the use of tips, take for granted that the machinery will only function well at the behest of the person operating it.

Smoking

Many, if not most, Brazilians smoke, and one rarely finds no-smoking areas in public places. No smoking signs are posted and generally observed in elevators and stores, but often the signs are not observed. Outside São Paulo people smoke anywhere, except perhaps in a movie theater. Few Brazilians would ask another to stop smoking, fearing the smoker would become angry and "probably wouldn't stop smoking anyway." A Brazilian proverb illustrates this attitude: *Os incomodados é que se mudem,* meaning, "He who feels uncomfortable should move, not the one doing whatever." Most Brazilians do not smoke during a meal, only after the *cafezinho* or occasionally during it.

Clubs

Public facilities like swimming pools, tennis courts, even camping facilities in a park are much less common in Brazil than in the United States. Facilities offered through private clubs and available only to members are much preferred. Like American tennis clubs, these sport clubs are often associated with a specific sport, though a club might offer several facilities to members. Some clubs combine high membership fees with a required approval of members before one joins and are consequently fairly exclusive. The most elite clubs are probably jockey clubs for horse racers. Tennis and golf clubs are generally regarded as upper and upper-middle class clubs.

Other clubs are less exclusive. Soccer or *futebol* clubs are probably the most popular among the majority of the middle class. Clubs may be organized around economic, occupational, or ethnic interests, or they may be purely social. Some municipal and state governments have organized clubs for young people similar to Y.W./Y.M.C.A. or to Boys Clubs of America. Clubs exist on all social levels, and much socializing takes place in them. Special parties like wedding receptions and other major family celebrations may be held there by a particular member, and clubs sponsor parties for members for major holidays like Christmas, New Year's, and *Carnaval.*

Potpourri

The first impression the North American generally receives of urban Brazil is one of confusion and noise. Part of this stems from the nature of city life anywhere, for most Americans in Brazil visit Rio, São Paulo, and other large urban centers. Part, though, is because of attitudes and behaviors that are specifically Brazilian, many of which seem contradictory to the North American. Traffic, for instance, is extremely congested in the cities. Drivers often ignore stop signs and stop lights. Drivers honk their horns if they notice other drivers using their headlights after dark in the city; urban drivers in Brazil use only the parking lights after dark. Buses usually take the right-of-way regardless of traffic or pedestrians. Drivers, especially taxi drivers, roll down their windows to shout their anger and may perform a gesture which looks similar to the North American "O.K." but is in fact obscene (see figure 49). Pedestrians are expected to avoid traffic rather than vice versa, and one American told of being advised to cross streets from mid-block, "where you only have two directions of traffic to worry about." At the same time, Brazilians like to help others, and if a stranger asks directions on the street, a Brazilian will not only give verbal directions, but may very well go along to be sure the directions were understood. One Brazilian told of being stranded in an airport by a cancelled flight, when a fellow passenger invited her home to spend the night, a doubly hospitable invitation in Brazil, where one's family and family life are considered to be very private matters. Drivers signal a car behind them whether or not the road is clear for passing. A left turn signal means the road is clear; a right turn signal means it is not. Flashing lights mean a policeman is in the area, and a flash from low beams to high beams means the car behind wants to pass.

As described in an earlier chapter, small booths on the street corners sell sandwiches, ice cream, and juices. Since Brazilians rarely eat anything while walking in the street, most booths have chairs, stools, benches, or at least an area where one can stand to eat a sandwich or ice cream. Brazilians are surprised by North American habits of eating on the street or eating while driving a car. Chewing gum on the street is likewise considered bad manners. Brazilians are surprised by the number of things we eat from or with our hands, such as sandwiches, which a Brazilian would eat with a knife and fork, or at least would wrap in a napkin. They also, however, toss the napkin on the ground when done eating, as they toss empty cups or bottles, paper, or cigarette butts on the ground. City streets are cleaned every day, so people are not concerned with what the North American describes as a litter problem. When carrying things in public, Brazilians wrap the item in paper or carry it in a bag.

DOING BUSINESS in BRAZIL

Nowhere do the differences between Brazil and North America appear more strongly than in the business world, partly because of the differences themselves, and partly because the business person has much more at stake financially and professionally, if not emotionally, than the casual visitor or the exchange student. Brazilians characteristically do not love work for its own sake. A Brazilian stereotype of North Americans is that "you love to work, and business comes first; pleasure and family life are of secondary importance."[1] The North American often blunders when negotiating in the Brazilian business world, largely because many of the qualities esteemed by his North American associates—aggressive confrontation of problems, an eager offering of suggestions and solutions, and a desire to "get straight to the point"—are precisely the qualities a Brazilian finds disquieting and even offensive. By the same token, the North American finds himself frustrated and culturally stymied by what he perceives as inefficiency and needless bureaucracy in the Brazilian system. Americans tend to approach business as a system of rules and procedures, whereas Brazilians often approach business as a particular kind of social interaction.

Part of the difficulty stems from the very different concepts of time held by each culture, differences which affect almost every aspect of life. As described on page 13, Edward T. Hall designates the two systems as monochronic or M-time, characteristic of North Americans, and polychronic or P-time, characteristic of Latin Americans generally. M-timers make schedules and follow them. Promptness is a virtue, tardiness a fault. M-time is divided into small units, so things can be dealt with individually. P-timers value people and problems over schedules and often deal with things simultaneously.[2] As with other aspects of Brazilian life, increasing industrialization with its time clocks and schedules has affected the Brazilian concept of time in areas like São Paulo. Still, the North American who insists on rigid schedules and prompt behavior is frequently frustrated in Brazil.

Because a Brazilian rarely arrives early, appointments are often delayed. One Brazilian businessman estimated fifteen to twenty minutes delay as standard, with "traffic" being the standard explanation, and another observed that one businessman arriving precisely on time might find the other not yet ready.

The Brazilian method of dealing with this unpredictability is to schedule appointments in one's office, so one can work while waiting, or agree to meet in the other's office, where he must appear sooner or later and where the secretary can acknowledge that the other kept the appointment. Even if the appointment is scheduled over lunch or cocktails, it is wise to arrange to meet in one or the other's office rather than in a restaurant or bar, "where you might never catch up with the other person." North Americans must give up the habit of scheduling full days with several appointments in the morning and several in the afternoon. Business is just not done that way in Brazil. In general, business dealings are more relaxed and people are not accustomed to rushing from one appointment to the next. One morning appointment and one afternoon appointment may very well fill the day. Another Brazilian business practice that North Americans find disquieting is dealing with several people simultaneously instead of individually in separate appointments. Brazilian business people, particularly public officials, are accustomed to dealing with several people and several issues at once, and to do so does not mean one issue or one person is less important and not worthy of individual attention. It is simply doing business, Brazilian style.

Besides, or perhaps because of, these different attitudes toward punctuality, Brazilians also take a very different approach to the general question of "doing business." A North American, who believes that "time is money," wants to "get down to business" or "get down to brass tacks"; he admires someone who can "get to the heart of the matter" and "hit the nail on the head." Such tactics will probably lead to a frustrated impasse in Brazil, where two people need to lay the proper social groundwork before any negotiations begin. One rarely, if ever, goes directly to a problem in business interactions. Preliminary socializing is imperative to establish a comfortable social climate of common backgrounds, interests, or associates, and if the chemistry is wrong, business may end before the American is aware it has begun. To discuss a problem, parties need to be in tune. One person barging in with a suggestion or question before the time is right ignores an important first step and risks immediate rejection. A bold frontal attack will likely be quietly but soundly defeated. A good example of this sort of interaction is the following description, provided by a Brazilian businesswoman, of checking the references of a prospective employee:

> Brazilians are very compassionate and will try to give the best possible picture of what happened. You should try to get references in face-to-face situations, push for specific details, "just between the two of us." The best way is to take someone to lunch, spend an hour and a half, establish rapport. At the very end of the lunch, do business, letting the senior person bring the subject up again.

One vital element in establishing rapport with business associates is the intermediary, the contact. Appointments are almost always made through an intermediary, and business people should try to establish contacts before leaving the U.S., so they can carry letters of introduction and perhaps of recommendation to Brazil. A good suggestion from a businesswoman whose job requires much traveling between Brazil and the United States was to carry the contact's business card with "Hello, this is my friend_____ "or "Mr._____ sent me here" written on the back. Plan on contacting people who can put you in touch with other people. Introductions are essential to doing business in Brazil, and the individual who simply sends a resume or appears in an office is not likely to accomplish much. The need for a contact or introduction also applies outside strict business dealings. As one North American observed, "If you know somebody, that's the key to everything in Brazil." Most Brazilians, as well as most North Americans who have spent much time in Brazil, have stories of the complicated procedures involved in any kind of official paperwork. In many cases, one needs to hire a *despachante* (literally, a dispatcher, one who does things with dispatch), a person who specializes in bureaucratic procedures and who knows who to see, when, where, and how. A North American college student told of encountering great difficulty using a Brazilian university archive, until he found *um jeito*. The Brazilian phrase means a way, a skill or an aptitude, and is frequently used in the general sense of working out a solution. A frequent solution in Brazil is to find a contact, someone to recommend or put in a good word.

Along the same lines, employers often hire friends and family over outsiders, regardless of skills or experience. A Brigham Young University study summarizes the issue well:

> The typical Brazilian family is much more closely knit than is the typical American family. To a Brazilian there isn't anything more important than his family. This includes not only his parents and brothers and sisters but also his aunts and uncles, cousins, and godparents and other "adopted" kin. With this realization, it isn't difficult to understand that when a Brazilian finds himself in an influential position he considers at once his responsibilities to help improve the positions in life of his family and friends. He attempts to *dar um jeito* to get his second cousin a job with his firm or to arrange a contract between his firm and his brother-in-law's factory.
>
> We in the United States are well acquainted with the idea that knowing the right people is very helpful in our endeavors to be successful. In Brazil this idea assumes ever larger proportions. When a Brazilian wants to get ahead in the world, one of the first things he does is to affiliate himself with someone or something that is already "ahead." If he has relatives in this position, so much the better. If not, he will appeal to a friend or a relative of a friend.[3]

Status, defined both by position/rank and salary and often by the length of time one has spent with the job or company, determines much in business interactions. In formal business dealings, the senior party, if male, is addressed as *Senhor* with his family name, unless the junior person is male and older, in which case both would be *Senhor*. Businesswomen are addressed as *Senhora* with the family name; outside business circles, women are addressed as *Dona* with the first name. A person with a degree or any person of superior status, is addressed as *doutor*, "doctor." Higher status people tend to arrive at work and to stay at work later than the standard workday hours (often eight to six with two hours for lunch). Having a secretary place a call or answer the telephone reflects a higher status, and if both the caller and the recipient have secretaries, the junior person would get on the line first. In regards to punctuality, higher status means more flexibility. A junior person must not keep a senior person waiting. If a junior person has waited an hour or longer, he might call the senior person's office, asking the secretary if the senior person has left and perhaps giving his apologies then, after making sure the secretary knows he has waited. In any business transaction, the junior person should never directly disagree with the senior. As in the United States, one's office also reflects one's status. Shared offices are quite common and space is a luxury. Generally only the higher positions have private offices, and the larger the office, the higher the status. Doors on offices also reflect privacy and high status. Desks and chairs, even in shared offices, are considered the "territory" of the person who works at them. Related to this sense of territory is office decor. Offices of public servants generally have few if any personal items like photographs or plants. In private business, employees might bring in personal items to decorate desks or offices, but many Brazilians are surprised by the extent to which North Americans personalize their offices, "as though you lived there."

Social relationships within offices in Brazil also reflect a concern with status. A high level employee or an employer would probably not take a lower level employee to lunch unless it were a special occasion, perhaps a department or staff lunch. Likewise, a junior person probably would not invite a senior person out for lunch, lest the invitation be interpreted as an attempt to ingratiate or ask a favor. However, a much lower level employee might ask a much higher level employee (i.e., janitor to company president) to his home for dinner, and if the higher level person accepts, it will be a big occasion and the junior person will invite family, friends, and neighbors. In this situation, the senior person should not accept immediately but should wait until the offer has been repeated several times (here one needs to distinguish between the vague "sometime" invitation which requires only a vague response and the direct invitation which requires either an acceptance or an explanation). When the senior person does accept, he should specify that he has another appointment at a certain time, or "the meal may go on forever." Offices mark holidays like Christmas with a small party, and business men exchange Christmas baskets filled with wines, cheeses, and nuts. Birthdays are generally not celebrated in offices, though colleagues and peers go to lunch, dinner, or for a beer to celebrate special events or just to socialize. A foreigner in an office might not be included in such things, not through any intentional exclusiveness but just because Brazilians might not take the initiative to introduce themselves. The foreigner should feel free to introduce himself.

Social life in a Brazilian office does involve some restrictions that a North American might easily trespass upon. Some of these involve conversational prohibitions: one should not ask about salary, or marital status, or a person's family unless the other person has brought up the subject. Brazilian home life is very sheltered from office life. It is reserved for close friends and family, and business acquaintances generally do not fit into those categories. One would probably not invite business colleagues home to dinner, though one might invite those colleagues to dinner in a restaurant. One should not telephone a business associate at home until given the phone number and told such a phone call would be welcome. Spouses might have absolutely no dealings with business associates, and a wife may not know her husband's salary. North Americans find this separation of home and office surprising, and many are hurt or put off by what they interpret as a lack of hospitality from Brazilian coworkers. North Americans, after all, often form their social friends from their business friends and do invite people into their homes very casually. The Brazilian reservation regarding home life is in no way a gesture of inhospitality but is an indication of and a protective device for the tightly knit Brazilian family.

Coffee breaks are very different in Brazilian offices, though the precise nature of the coffee break depends, of course, upon the individual business. Coffee is served every two hours in public offices and in many businesses, and it is offered whenever one has a visitor or meets a client. The coffee is a dark roast, brewed very strong, and served with lots of sugar in a demitasse cup, hence the name *cafezinho*, little coffee. High officials and executives might have a waiter to serve coffee. Some businesses have a small cart that goes through the office with coffee and snacks, and these might be free. The coffee break is a time to set work aside and relax. Some offices employ office boys or errand boys who perform small jobs and serve coffee. A business person should not assume that the office secretary makes the coffee. Several business people viewed making coffee as the "function of the waiter" and below the duty of a secretary. One young woman who had worked as a secretary told of her employer asking her to serve coffee, whereupon she asked him if she would receive a tip. At the same time, one should not volunteer to make or serve the coffee oneself, as that might suggest the secretary is not doing her job. The secretary is the proper channel for finding the correct procedures regarding coffee in the office, and the newcomer would be wise to ask.

Brazilians often spot North Americans almost immediately by the differences in dress, particularly in women's dress. An American business woman who plans to work in Brazil should redo or at least adjust her wardrobe. Dress codes are discussed in detail in chapter five, but following are few points with particular application to business people.

The importance of dressing fashionably cannot be over-stressed. Brazilians are extremely fashion conscious, and fashions change rapidly in Brazil—every year for women, and almost as frequently for men. A sensible approach would be to start with a basic wardrobe of quality classic items and then play with trendy accessories, and for women, blouses, shoes, and handbags. Styles for both men and women follow French and Italian models. One will have no trouble determining current fashions as that will be the only thing available in most stores.

Businesswomen wear dresses and skirts, and perhaps carry a jacket in warmer areas or warmer seasons. Blouses can be short sleeved, as can jackets, and necklines on blouses are often lower and more open than is common in the United States. Women wear cotton and lots of silk—nothing gives an American away faster than synthetic fabrics, especially polyester. Brazilian women generally use more makeup than North American women, and businesswomen are no exception. Manicured hands are very important for both women and men, and women take great care with their feet, also.

Businessmen in Brazil are also very conscious of presenting a neat and stylish appearance. Men working for the government must wear a suit and tie. Excutives wear three-piece suits, and the average office worker wears a suit. Shirts are starched and pressed, *never* short sleeved (a short-sleeved white shirt is a sure sign of an American, as are white socks), generally linen or silk, and often bright, solid colors. Suits tend to be lighter colors, bieges and grays, especially in warmer climates, and shirts, jackets, and slacks are cut tighter than North American styles. Men often leave the first two or three buttons open on a sport shirt and never wear undershirts. Jewelry for men is common—I.D. bracelets, heavy chains with a cross or religious medal, as well as wristwatches (older men might carry a pocket watch), rings, cuff links, and tie pins. Accessories like belts are leather, and Brazilian business-men carry briefcases on business occasions, large clutch-type wallets on informal occasions. Some higher level businessmen have dropped the use of the briefcase, believing it to be a mark of the average white-color worker. Hair should be trimmed and neat. Trimmed moustaches are common, but beards are generally not favored and if worn would be well trimmed.

A word about businesswomen in Brazil. North American women often have difficulty dealing with the *macho* attitude found in Latin cultures generally and certainly present in Brazil. The woman doing business in Brazil and the wife accompanying her husband on business in Brazil must learn to work within the Brazilian system if they want to succeed there. If contacts and introductions are important for a man, they are critical for a woman. Brazilian men do not expect to see women in executive and managerial positions. Although women occupy all levels of the working world and have for some time, and though many attain professional careers in dentistry, teaching, and some branches of law, the majority of women in the business world are secretaries. The woman doing business with a man must be particularly careful not to appear too aggressive but to establish rapport and, if possible, let the suggestions come from the man, or at least appear to come from the man. A man's image is extremely important in Brazil, and the North American businesswoman who is determined to behave as an equal will have difficulty negotiating business, if she is able to negotiate at all. Businesswomen and wives may drink, but they should choose wine and hard liquor rather than beer and should absolutely never be drunk in public. A woman should expect to be flirted with and approached, and should refuse such overtures firmly but graciously. A wife should never flirt with her husband's business associates. Finally, and plainly at this point, businesswomen and wives should simply not press the issue of women's rights and should not present a liberated front in Brazil, at least not if their goals include successful business negotiations in a country that is traditionally male dominated. Overassertiveness closes doors to women in Brazil.

Notes

1. Jose Honorio Rodrigues, *The Brazilians: Their Character and Aspirations*, trans. Ralph Edward Dimmick (Austin: Univ. of Texas Press, 1967), p. 51.

2. *Beyond Culture* (Garden City, New York: Anchor Press/Doubleday, 1976), p. 14ff.

3. *People of Brazil* (Provo, Utah: Brigham Young University Language and Intercultural Research Center, 1977), p. 12.

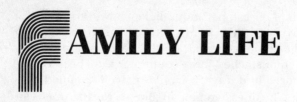

FAMILY LIFE

Brazilian family life differs greatly from North American family life, though as with so many other aspects of Brazilian society, increasing industrialization in the South is altering many of the traditional patterns and creating home and family patterns more like those of the United States. The family, particularly in the upper and upper-middle classes, forms a critical social unit in Brazil and exerts a far greater influence on family members than is typical in North America. Brazilians, while they admire and enjoy aspects of North American independence and privacy, feel that American families have no roots or depth. They are surprised by the North American parent's eager concern that children go away from home for college and take part-time jobs in college and sometimes even in high school. North Americans stress individual independence and see the son's or daughter's move out of the house, often described as "leaving the nest," as an important step toward adult status. Not so in Brazil, where living alone is not a sign of independence, but a sign that one lacks family. Brazilians show dismayed surprise at the commonness of retirement and nursing homes in North America and see in them a lack of concern for the aged and for the family unit as a whole.

The extended family living pattern predominates in Brazil, and "extended" can include grandparents, aunts, uncles, cousins, and second cousins. Children remain at home until they marry, even if this means until age twenty-seven or twenty-eight. If a young couple cannot afford their own home when they marry, they live with one set of parents. When children establish their own households, they try to settle close to the parents and continue to visit them regularly, at least once a week. The only reason a son or daughter might leave home before marriage would be to take a job or attend a university in a different city, but most Brazilians try to avoid such a move. As noted in the Overview, second, third, and fourth cousins often marry, thus strengthening the family unit by combining family and social spheres. This family network fills the place of nursing and retirement homes for aged relatives. If both parents are living, they might share a house or apartment to themselves, but if only one parent remains, he or she most likely lives with a child or with another relative. Most Brazilians do not accept retirement homes, seeing them as an unpleasant necessity for those unfortunates who do not have family. One man from Belém summarized the attitude: "If I send my father there, my son will send me there." Each generation cares for the preceding generation and expects the same care from the subsequent generation.

Americans should be aware that this extended family pattern is characteristic of middle and upper class families, but does not hold true for many Brazilian families which lack the economic resources to support it. Single parent and nuclear families are becoming increasingly common in the cities, especially in the *favelas*. One indirect result of the economic infeasibility of the traditional extended family is the large numbers of homeless *pivetes* or urchins who roam city streets. Americans seeing these children and adolescents sometimes stereotype Brazilians as callous; the problem is not that Brazilians do not care, but that social services have not caught up to the problem in Brazil.

Being accustomed to this pattern, most Brazilians are not accustomed to being alone for any length of time, and the notion of "needing time alone" strikes them as "very American" and as indicative of depression or unhappiness. One man told of his uncle who, displeased with living alone, took two of his maid's sons to live with him. He had company, and the boys had room, board, and an education. The boys had the status of friends—not family, but certainly not servants or boarders. An American anthropologist in Brazil with his wife told of neighbors who, knowing the wife was gone for the day, sent their two children over to keep him company, and gently reproved the wife later for leaving her husband alone all day. If a young person leaves his parents' city to work or attend school, he will probably not live alone in his new location but will live with relatives or room-mates.

Brazilians are accustomed to the sharing of physical space. At home, a Brazilian is surrounded by family, perhaps friends, and probably maids. Individual children do not necessarily have separate bedrooms, and though older children are generally separated by sex, siblings often share bedrooms and perhaps beds.

Children occupy a special place within the extended family. In the words of one Brazilian, "Children are venerated." In public, strangers who may or may not address the parents may praise a child, perhaps patting his head, tugging his cheek, or gently squeezing an arm. Married couples are expected to have children soon, and families are large by North American standards. Parents take their children just about everywhere they go, unless a host specifically excludes children in the invitation (in which case some parents may not attend), or unless the event is a late one. If parents do not take their children along, they leave a relative (a grandparent or an elder sibling), or perhaps a maid in charge. Babysitters are virtually unknown in Brazil, largely because the extended family allows for much sharing of the childcare responsibilities, but also because families that can afford to do so hire a *babá*, a nursemaid whose sole job is to watch the children. Although Brazilians find the North American family a much weaker unit than their own, they are surprised at the amount of time an American mother spends with her children and at her total responsibility for them. At parties and dinner parties, Brazilian children sit at the same table and entertain themselves in the same room with adults. One Brazilian woman was horrified by American playpens, describing them as "little jails" (again, one must remember that the upper or middle class Brazilian family often contains a large number of people to watch over toddlers). Infants and young children are held almost constantly, and should a child cry, family members rush to take care of the problem. The notions of letting a child "cry it out" or "get it out of his system" are totally foreign to Brazilian parents.

Brazilians generally do not discipline their children in public. Physical punishment, such as spanking, is viewed as harsh and regarded with disfavor. An unruly child might be taken out of the room or away from the gathering until he displays more appropriate behavior, but Brazilian parents might simply ignore what an American finds distracting behavior. A Brazilian parent tries to avoid putting children into situations where discipline might be a problem, such as expecting young children to behave quietly at church, in a formal restaurant, or any other context where they are likely to become bored, inattentive, or possibly disruptive.

Because they are so often in social situations, Brazilian children and young adults are used to interacting with large numbers of people of various ages. "In Brazil, kids ease into adulthood," perhaps because they are around adults so much of the time. Children enjoy the freedom to go in and out of neighbors' houses as they please, and in their own homes they sit on a visitor's lap, or hug and maybe kiss him or her. Brazilians describe Brazilian children as "spoiled," but they do not see that as a bad thing.

Other family roles are fairly well defined. Women, many with the help of maids, do nearly all the housework. One student remarked that even when she was in the United States going to school and living with a group of Brazilians, the men expected the women to take care of the household chores. Men may help with heavier chores around the house, but for the most part, the home is the woman's responsibility. Preschool children are not expected to help around the house. When children reach school age, their responsibilities are to study and do their homework. Education is valued highly, particularly by upper and middle class Brazilians, and many who can afford to do so send their adolescent children to private boarding schools *(internatos)*. Girls begin helping with household chores around the age of fourteen and are generally brought up more strictly than boys, with less freedom to keep late hours or go out alone. Young men are also freer to move out of the home than are young women. Parents, as well as other family members, expect to know where children and teenagers are going, why, with whom, and when they will return. Parents, family members, and even neighbors ask questions about an individual's friends or boyfriend. Such questions result in part from curiosity but in a larger part from concern.

Teenagers often socialize in groups, and groups frequently go out to the beaches, to a movie, to a party, or to a club. Even when they begin dating (usually around age seventeen, though girls particularly may begin to talk of dating at fifteen or earlier), young people spend much of their time in groups. One Brazilian described this group socializing as "providing a pool from which to choose a steady partner," and described teenage dating as "more a pairing off within the group" than between individual couples. Dating relationships are not necessarily viewed as serious or long term, though if a boy visits a girl in her home, as opposed to pairing off within the group, the relationship is likely to be considered more seriously. Further, though early relationships may not be considered as serious in themselves, Brazilians are extremely couple oriented and teenage girls especially view having a boyfriend as a vital concern. Many families do not allow a teenage daughter to stay out after ten o'clock, due as much to concern over what neighbors will think as to actual dangers. The general Brazilian attitude is that girls and women must be protected. Teenage couples are usually chaperoned, if not by the group, then by another couple, a sister, or a cousin. "To chaperone" in Brazilian Portuguese is *segurar a vela*—to hold the candle.

Male and female roles are changing in Brazil, and the changes show clearly in the behavior of teenagers and young adults. One example of such change is the aggressive flirting, initiated by teenage girls in movie theaters, described on page 54. Another example comes from public bars, often regarded as unsuitable and sometimes as unsafe for unescorted women. One Brazilian woman in her early twenties told of going to bars without a male escort (though always with another woman or in a group of women) as a teenager. Although they viewed this as rebellious behavior and as something that elders would frown upon, they did not view it as dangerous behavior. Once in the bar, the woman should let the man take the initiative. "A very young woman might approach a man, ask him to dance, to have a drink, but only as a joke." After a man has asked a woman to join him, she might suggest he sit at her table, but the initial invitation should come from the man. By and large, however, as one woman in her early twenties observed, "Nowadays, teenage girls do just about everything the guys do." Another woman in her late twenties said that such was not the case when she was a teenager and is still not the case with her age group today.

Visiting in the Home

Family visits often occupy most Sundays for Brazilians. Grandparents, children, cousins, and in-laws gather at one house (which house might be determined by size, location, or family status), and people who are not family members generally do not make unannounced visits on Sunday. These visits are rarely prearranged or formally organized. Rather, family members gather, visit, eat a large meal between noon and two o'clock, visit through the afternoon and end the day with a light snack of leftovers from the noon meal. Since the visitors often bring their maids along, the day serves as a chance for the maids to visit with one another while watching over the children and helping with the meal. Brazilian teenagers may become impatient with the traditional Sunday visits and may slip away for an afternoon at the beach or with friends, but the Sunday visit is an important institution in most Brazilian families.

Perhaps because of the extended family living pattern, social occasions in the home are reserved for family and close friends. Much socializing takes place in clubs, at school, in bars and *barzinhos*, and in the streets. One might receive visitors in the garden of the house, but Brazilians show much more regard for the privacy of the home than do North Americans. A young man from São Paulo described knowing his girlfriend for nearly a year before he visited her in her home. Such reservation strikes the North American as unfriendly, since we invite people into our homes fairly casually, but it is in fact a sign of respect for the family. Brazilians often invite friends to dine in a restaurant or bar, and such an invitation is a genuine gesture of hospitality and friendship.

This respect for the privacy of home life shows up in the general plan of upper and middle class houses. (Current inflation is such that only the wealthier Brazilians purchase houses. Most urban Brazilians live in apartments, in which case the following would not apply.) The house is often surrounded by a large garden, so the house itself sits at some distance from the street. A fence or wall separates the garden from the street, and one should announce his presence at the gate, before entering the fenced garden. Electric bells or buzzers are fairly common now, but in some areas, particularly smaller towns and rural areas, one still finds the traditional manner of announcing oneself at the gate by clapping, perhaps calling "*Ô de casa*" at the same time. The phrase means roughly "Is anybody home?" The clapping serves to notify people in the house of a visitor's presence before he has approached the door. If the clapping receives no response though the owner is clearly at home and simply did not hear it, you may approach the house, knocking on the door or ringing the bell when you reach the house. Doors are often quite literally open in Brazil, in which case you may again clap and call to give notice of your presence.

Brazilians generally do not "drop by" the homes of people they do not know well, such as casual acquaintances or business acquaintances. If a particular reason demands such a visit, one need not telephone first, but the visit should be kept short and might be conducted in the garden or patio rather than in the house itself. New neighbors, too, might introduce themselves across the garden gate. If food is served during such a visit, it might be brought to the garden from the house. North Americans invite people into their homes frequently and with relative ease, and interpret the lack of such invitations as a sign of unfriendliness. This interpretation is incorrect in Brazil, where the home is reserved for family and for a few very close friends.

A related misunderstanding concerns what North Americans have labelled the Brazilian habit of extending insincere invitations to visit. This statement results from two misunderstandings, the first being the Brazilian concern for pleasant and friendly interaction, which may result in profuse and casual general invitations or expressions of friendship. Such invitations and expressions (like *apareça,* "show up sometime," or *apareça lá em casa,* "show up at my house sometime") are *not* insincere. They stem from a genuine warmth and goodwill. They should not, however, be interpreted as firm invitations. A good rule of thumb is to gauge the expectation behind such an invitation by the specificity with which it is offered. If directions or an address are given with the invitation, or if a specific date and time are suggested, it is probably a firm engagement. The second misunderstanding stems from North Americans being alone in a foreign country, not knowing many people, and so putting more weight on casual relationships and statements than they would on home ground. We, too, tell casual acquaintances to "drop by sometime" and ask them to "come for dinner sometime" without considering ourselves firmly engaged. Such statements are motivated by a desire to make someone feel welcome and at ease.

If, however, one establishes a friendship with a Brazilian, visiting becomes a totally different matter. Brazilians visit friends regularly (one woman commented that a week between visits would be a long gap), and occasions for visiting can be planned or casual. One is perfectly free to "drop by" a friend's home and need not telephone in advance. Brazilians rarely telephone before casual visits and find the North American habit of doing so somewhat formal and cold, taking the spontaneity or surprise out of a visit. Visits tend to be lengthy by American standards, lasting at least an hour and maybe two. If a visitor knows beforehand a visit will be short, he should say so when he arrives; if it is clear that a visit is disruptive, the visitor should offer a reason for leaving after a short stay. An afternoon visit should end by five o'clock, so people can begin preparing dinner for seven. Evening visits begin late and extend late—sometimes far into the night by North American standards, particularly on the weekends. A visitor would not bring flowers or a gift, unless the visit marked some special event, like a birthday.

When a friend arrives, a Brazilian drops whatever he is doing to visit, even if he is busy with matters that a North American would consider to have precedence. A woman described a Brazilian friendship as "a constant sacrifice." One might hint about a pressing engagement or tomorrow's exam, but one would not ask a person to come back later or make any direct statement to indicate that business was more important than a visit from a friend. Brazilians are hurt and offended by the North American assumption that business comes first and is therefore a legitimate reason to curtail a social call. Likewise, a visit from a friend is a legitimate excuse for lateness in Brazil. A guest takes precedence over a telephone call as well. The presence of a visitor provides a legitimate excuse for ending the call or for ignoring the bell, as a Brazilian would not leave a guest to attend to the telephone.

A visitor arriving during a meal will be pressed to stay and share it. Again, if the visit is obviously creating an uncomfortable situation, the visitor should give a reason for leaving and should leave. Generally, however, a friend would not feel the least uncomfortable or cause any disruption if his visit were to coincide with a meal. When invited to stay and share a meal, a visitor should refuse the first offer. This refusal allows the host to show his generosity and goodwill without risking embarrassment by an obvious lack of food or any other difficulty. The invitation will be repeated, at which time the visitor may accept. One Brazilian remarked that she advised newly arrived Brazilians that "You're in America now; you'll only be asked once." If a refusal is intended as final, it should be accompanied by an explanation, "I just ate," for example, or "I am meeting someone for dinner later." An unexplained refusal may make the host wonder "why a friend isn't comfortable enough to share a meal." At the same time, some Brazilians use the phrase *Não faça cerimônia* or *Eu não faço cerimônia* ("Don't stand on ceremony," or "I won't stand on ceremony") to dispense with the exchange of request/refusal outlined above.

"Portuguese hospitality" means that a host(ess) will always offer food or drink or both to visitors, and again, though the visitor might refuse and probably should refuse the first offer, he should have an explanation if he intends a firm refusal. As mentioned earlier, "Thanks" indicates a refusal in Brazil, and "No, thank you" is considered rather too blunt to be polite. A visitor should probably accept something, as a host(ess) is likely to continue offering various things in an attempt to find something to please the guest. Coffee will probably be offered, less often tea. Soft drinks or fruit juice might also be offered. Sweets—cookies, cake, or candy—are likely to be offered as well. A Brazilian host or hostess will always offer something, as the sharing of food provides an important outward sign of friendship and goodwill, and the importance of sharing food increases as the economic and/or social status of the host(ess) decreases. Upper-class Brazilians might be less concerned with whether or not a visitor shares their food, but less affluent Brazilians will be extremely concerned to offer their hospitality and "poor people will be troubled if you do not accept. They will think it's a reflection on their poverty." Food is served in the living or dining room, the kitchen being reserved for maids and for very close friends.

In the past, coffee was served at the close of a visit, and visitors would depart after finishing their cup. This custom is not necessarily followed today, and the serving of food and coffee depends upon the time of the visitor's arrival and the expected length of the stay. Still, a Brazilian host(ess) would probably not serve coffee immediately upon a guest's arrival. Actual leave taking may be protracted, marked by the same negotiation as marked the offering of food. A host(ess) will urge guests to stay, saying "*É cedo!*" ("It's early!") no matter what the hour, and a guest should probably accede to the first request. A guest should, however, be sensitive to the fact that a host(ess) will urge the guest to stay no matter how late the hour is, and should time his departure accordingly. A host(ess) will escort guests to the door and will not go back into the house until the departing guests are out of sight, and might escort guests to their cars and watch them drive away. Conversation will continue during leave taking—one couple told of talking for almost an hour between their decision to leave and their final departure. One reason behind such extended departures is that the departure of one guest may cause others to feel obliged to leave also. Hence an early departure could affect an entire gathering, or at least cause noticeable strain. Such strain will be eased only if a visitor has made his early departure clear from the beginning and offered a concrete explanation for it.

Maids

Upper class and upper-middle class Brazilians employ women as maids to do the cooking and the heavy housework and may employ a male gardener as well. If one lives in the country, one might hire a married couple to fill these functions, the gardener serving also as a guard and perhaps as a chauffeur. In the past, maids' wages were not regulated, but now maids must be paid minimum wage, so fewer people can afford to hire them. Further, increasing industrialization in the South is providing more job opportunities for the unskilled, so fewer women are willing to work as maids, a job that may restrict personal freedom. Many Brazilians employ maids who come to the home once or twice a week to do heavy cleaning; others employ maids who come in daily, and many hire a maid who lives in the home and works six days a week in return for room, board, and a salary. Maids are generally hired to perform specific tasks and may be annoyed or offended if asked to perform a different job. A *cozinheira* cooks, an *arrumadeira* does housework, and a *babá* tends to children.

Being a maid is considered a low-status occupation in Brazil, though different skills command higher salaries and greater status (cooks, for example, are often accorded a higher status than a maid who cleans). College students in Brazil would never take summer or part-time jobs as maids (or construction workers, or any of the manual labor jobs with which many American students finance an education). Such roles are generally filled by people from lower economic classes, often people who have moved into the city from the country or to the South from the North. Girls might begin to work as maids at age sixteen and might continue to serve as maids when they marry and have children. Maids often move from job to job, looking for better wages and better situations, with a year and a half to two years being an average stay. At the same time, some Brazilians have the same maid for many years, in which case a particularly close relationship may develop between maid and family.

The typical relationship between employer and maid is a mixture of paternalistic regard and businesslike efficiency, though the precise relationship depends upon the length of time the maid has been in the family. Many Brazilians encourage their maids to attend school and to study, and a maid might approach the head of the household to ask advice on personal matters. An employer should remember a maid and perhaps her children on birthdays, at Christmas, and at Easter. One might bring a small *lembrança* (gift) to a maid when returning from a trip, and, if the maid has been in the family for some time, might provide some extra financial help for unexpected personal difficulties or to help start a long-term project. Outgrown or out-of-fashion clothing is often passed along to maids. A houseguest should always leave a small gift for the maid or maids at the end of a visit. The gift may be cash, left with the host or hostess to be given to the maid. A guest might deliver a cash gift personally, offering an apology for not having had the time to purchase a gift.

North Americans generally are not used to dealing with maids, particularly with live-in maids (hence our familiar jokes about cleaning up for the cleaning lady), and as a result are known for "not being assertive enough" with maids. Generally, maids do not expect to be treated as social equals and are amused (though sometimes offended) by North Americans performing the maid's duty for her—running to fix oneself a quick breakfast or make a pot of tea. One should always be polite with a maid, giving orders firmly and clearly, and should be prepared to reprimand firmly but without anger if a maid does not do as asked. The social distance between men and maids is greater than that between women and maids. Several young women said they might watch TV with their maids, and one married woman said she often watched TV with her maid when her husband was away. If one should meet one's maid in a public place (though such a meeting is apparently unlikely), one would say hello but would probably not stop to chat. A woman should be careful not to behave too informally with male servants, as it might be interpreted as loose behavior.

Live-in maids have their own quarters, consisting of a small room, a closet, and a bathroom. If a maid has a child, the child might live with her, though most live-in maids are single women without children. Maids do most of the cooking and eat the same food the family eats, though they do not eat at the same table and may, in fact, be busy serving the food. Conversations are somewhat restricted, though not terribly so, when a maid is in the room.

When hiring a maid, one can advertise or use the Brazilian equivalent of an employment agency, but the preferred method is to ask friends to ask their maids if they know anyone wanting a position. Candidates should be interviewed, references checked, and duties carefully explained. Salaries depend upon a number of factors—special duties, size of family, location of home in the city—and the current inflation rate makes estimates impossible, but that information should be available from acquaintances and agencies in Brazil. An employer should expect to train a maid, spending anywhere from a week to a month teaching her the specific details of one's own routine.

▤ INDEPENDENT GESTURES

Laurence Wylie introduces his study of gestures with the observation that "Perhaps there should be a warning on the cover. DANGEROUS! USE ONLY AS DIRECTED! Gesturing may get you into trouble or at least put you in difficult situations, if you do not know the cultural implications of different gestures."[1] Learning to gesture involves learning rules of context as well as specific meanings, and gestures, like vocabulary, may involve connotations not readily apparent through dictionary meanings. Thus the foreigner might be advised to limit the use of gestures until personal observations of Brazilians using Brazilian gestures has helped to fill in some of these subtleties of meaning.

Brazilians use a large number of independent gestures or emblems—that is, gestures with specific meanings which may include but do not require verbal explanation or support. Further, Brazilians use gestures frequently, far more frequently than the average North American, whose lack of gestures makes him seem somewhat cold and aloof to a Brazilian. A woman from Belo Horizonte observed, "I am more comfortable when people use their hands." Another woman, from São Paulo, noted that "Brazilians use their hands a lot, as if they were conducting, holding a baton. My hands are part of my oral communication." Mark Knapp warns his readers that "nonverbal communication is so inextricably bound up with verbal aspects of the communication process that we can only separate them artificially."[2] Readers of this volume should likewise be cautioned that the following catalogue reflects an artificial separation of gestures for the sake of study and reference, just as a dictionary reflects the artificial separation of words.

Gesture is considered a fairly informal communicative device in Brazil, so although gestures are used often, they are not used everywhere by everyone. Some gestures reflect cultural trends or styles, and so are used widely for a short time and then disappear, or are associated with a particular area. Some gestures are appropriate only to certain age and/or sex groups; their use by members of other groups (a man, for example using a child's gesture, or a woman using a man's gesture) would be interpreted as either joking or as very odd behavior. An interesting observation came from a Brazilian-American who thought that Brazilian men gestured more than Brazilian women. "Gestures are powerful. A gesture is a performance, and the focus is on the person performing, gesturing." As observers like Albert Mehrabian and Erving Goffman have pointed out, status *is* a factor in kinesic and gestural forms of behavior.

Limitations of time and space prevent an exhaustive dictionary of Brazilian gestures. We have limited this chapter to gestures not mentioned elsewhere in the handbook which are uncommon in the North American gesture repertoire or which exist with different meanings in the different cultures. In photographing specific gestures, we have tried to provide illustrations that are both clear and typical, not always easy since many of the gestures involve motion and no two individuals gesture in precisely the same way. Verbal description attempts to fill in the gaps. For readers of Portuguese, *História dos Nossos Gestos* by Luís da Câmara Cascudo provides a fine historical study of a large number of Brazilian gestures.

Attention-Getters (figures 10–12)

Several gestures serve primarily to attract attention to oneself or to interrupt a conversation. One common gesture indicating "I want to talk to you" involves pointing directly at one's mouth with the index finger (figure 10), using a short, fluttering motion. The finger does not touch the lips. Somewhat less common is a style of beckoning which can mean "I want to talk to you" or simply "Come here" (figure 11). Position of the forearm ranges from vertical to outstretched horizontal, and the palm can be open and held forward or downward. The fingers alone are flexed, not the entire hand. North Americans can confuse this beckon with a wave of greeting. One Brazilian explained the gesture as "more logical" than the North American beckon, since a person walks on the ground, not though the air, as the North American beckon suggests. Another Brazilian characterized the gesture as "fishing for the person." Two gestures indicate "Telephone me." One is to imitate holding a telephone receiver to one's ear (figure 12), and the other uses one hand to make a cranking motion near the ear.

Behaving Brazilian

Figure 10
"I want to talk to you."

Figure 11
"Come here, I want
to talk to you."

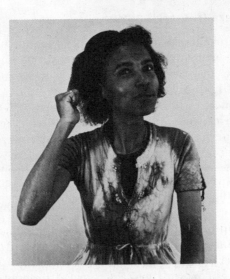

Figure 12
"Telephone me."

Two similar gestures mean "I want time" and can be used to interrupt a conversation. The palm is held flat, facing down, and is tapped either with the index finger or with the tips of the fingers on the other hand, as a referee asks for time out during a sports event. A common paralinguistic device for attracting attention is a hissing sound, subtle but penetrating, made by blowing through closed teeth and pursed lips, symbolized by "psiu psiu." Meaning "Come here," it might be used to call a friend, to call a waiter in a restaurant (though *not* in a formal restaurant), or by men on the street or the beach to attract the attention of a woman. The sound penetrates well, and one American described it as "a good way to call someone when 'Hey!' would be rude." It might also be used in a classroom or lecture situation to indicate displeasure or disagreement with a speaker.

Children's Gestures (figures 13–16)

Some gestures are used primarily by children or toward children, and their use by adults toward adults would be considered inappropriate except as joking behavior. One such gesture indicates truth, as North American children use "cross my heart." The Brazilian parallel uses crossed index fingers (figure 13) with the phrase *"juro"*—I swear. The crossed fingers are kissed and then the fingers might be reversed and kissed again. Women use this gesture as well as children. Linking little fingers (figure 14) indicates friendship and is the basis of a children's ritual to mark dissolution and reaffirmation of friendship. When two children are angry, they will link fingers and pull them apart, saying *"Tô de mal"*—"I am in bad with you" or "I am through with you." One child might use the free hand to split the linked fingers, or a third person might break the link. When the breach is repaired, the two will link little fingers again and twist their hands so as to touch thumbs, saying *"Tô de bem"*—"I am in good with you" or "I am in your good graces." Linking fingers is also used to indicate the placing of a bet. Two people placing a bet might link little fingers, saying "Let's bet on it," or might use the gesture on its own. This gesture might be used by men, women, or children.

The first portion of the routine described above might be accomplished by one person holding his hands in front of his body and about chest high, fingers interlocked and palms out. Pushing forward with the hands to separate fingers represents

Figure 13
"*Juro!*"—"I swear!"

Figure 14
Breaking a friendship; also, the placing of a bet.

Figure 15
Two people, things, or ideas are very close.

Figure 16
Adult to child, "Behave!"

the separation of friends. Another gesture used to indicate friendship or to indicate that two things are very close is to rub the index fingers together (figure 15). This gesture is used primarily by children, though it may be used by adults as well, and indicates a strong relationship, particularly between two people. Figure 16 represents the threat of a spanking and would be used by a parent to a child. The gesture could be used in jest, particularly if used between peers, but between parent and child usually constitutes genuine warning of disciplinary action. It would probably not be used in public as a genuine warning. Whether as joke or as warning, the shoe is shaken at the child. Other gestures used by adults to discipline children include drawing the thumb and index finger against the lips while blowing through closed teeth ("pss" as opposed to the North American "shhh"), both of which mean "Be quiet." Interestingly, the "shhh" sound used by North Americans to mean "Be quiet" indicates the anticipation of danger or punishment in Brazil. Gently twisting the ear of a disobedient child serves as a warning to behave. Disciplinary warning might be conveyed to a child through the snap of the index finger against the middle finger (cf. figure 22), or with the shaking of an index finger at the child, common also in North American gesture language. Parents might also use threat of the *bicho papão* (boogeyman) to discipline a young child.

Departure, Motion, and Speed (figures 17–22)

Making a fist and opening it quickly (figures 17 and 18) may be used in a variety of situations. Its general meaning is "Go away,"

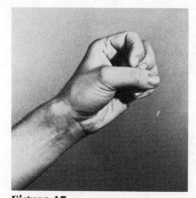

Figure 17
"Go away!"

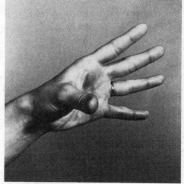

Figure 18
"Go away!"

but it could be used as a command, to tell a person to go away, reflexively, to describe one's own desire or intention to leave, or descriptively, to indicate a desire for a problem or a situation to go away. *Puxar o carro*, "to pull the car" or "to pull the cart" (figures 19 and 20) also means "Let's go." The fingers and palm of one open hand are brushed quickly across the other open palm, beginning at the heel of the hand and ending at the fingertips. The motion is quick and may involve the entire surface of each hand or only the fingertips. *Puxar o carro* implies a hasty departure, and may be used to show one thing moving faster than another or to emphasize speed. Another gesture meaning "Let's go" is to extend the hand forward at about waist level, palm open and facing upward, wrist loose, and to shake the palm from side to side (figure 21). The motion is quick, the implication being "Hurry up! Let's get out of here!" A paralinguistic device associated with speed but used for many situations involves a loud snapping noise made by extending the arm and hand, thumb and middle finger touching, index finger loose, and flicking the wrist so the index finger strikes the middle finger (figure 22). The sound is similar to a loud snap of the fingers. It could be used to cheer a team at a sports event or to encourage someone to hurry. It might also be used as a reaction to pain—after touching something hot— or to discipline a child. This gesture is difficult and sometimes painful for Americans to learn, though most Brazilians master it at an early age. Part of the trick seems to be relaxing the fingers while flicking the wrist.

Disbelief (figures 23–26)

One common gesture to indicate disbelief is to tug gently at the lower eyelid (figure 23). One might tug gently, several times, or pull the lid down and hold it down briefly. It could be used either to indicate disbelief ("You don't think I'm crazy enough to believe *that!*") or to warn someone to "watch out, keep your eyes open." Described as a "cute gesture" by one Brazilian, it would probably not be used if a person were seriously angry. *Papo furado* (figure 24) refers to a turkey's craw and means someone does not know what he is talking about. The backs of the fingers are tapped on the underside of the chin. Two variants of this gesture, both less common than the above, are tugging at the front of the neck with the thumb and index finger (figure 25), or pointing the index

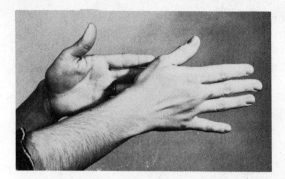

Figure 19
Puxar o carro,
indicates speed.

Figure 20
Puxar o carro,
indicates speed.

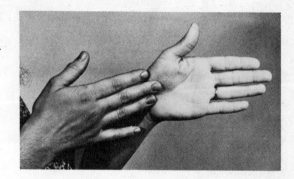

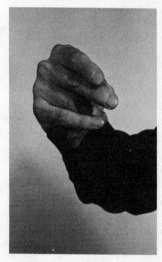

Figure 21
"Hurry up! Let's go!"

Figure 22
Indicates speed

finger at the jawbone while blowing out through pursed lips to make a hissing sound (figure 26). These three gestures are fairly rude and can mean something is a lie (*Isso é garganta*) in the sense of a tall tale or story. A North American equivalent would be

Figure 23
Indicates disbelief. Sometimes accompanied by *"Aquí oh!"*

Figure 24
Papo furado, "I don't know."
"He doesn't know."

Figure 25
Papo furado

Figure 26
Papo furado

"bull." A less common gesture indicating disbelief is tapping the lip gently with an index finger.

Good Luck (figures 27 and 28)

"Thumbs up" (figure 27) is seen frequently in Brazil and can be used to wish oneself or someone else good luck, or to indicate praise. This gesture is used where North Americans would use a circle made with the thumb and index finger, remaining fingers open (cf. figures 48 and 49), an obscene gesture in Brazil. The *figa* (figure 28), though *highly* obscene in many parts of the world, (Italy, for example), means "good luck" in Brazil. It is associated particularly with northern Brazil, especially Bahia, but is known throughout the country. While the *figa* is sometimes used as a gesture, one is more likely to encounter it as a good luck token— worn as a bracelet or necklace, carried as an amulet on a keychain, or hung on a door in a house. One might also encounter the expression *fazer figa* or *fazer figuinha* (to make a *figa* or to make a little *figa*), used like the American expression "I'll keep my fingers crossed." Brazilians use crossed fingers, as do North Americans, to wish for luck or to indicate the telling of a lie, and also use the customary "knocking on wood" to avoid bad luck. One might also indicate good luck by linking little fingers (fig. 14), the same gesture used by children to indicate friendship.

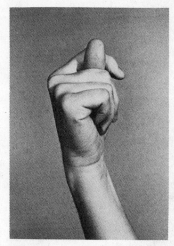

Figure 27
"Good luck!"

Figure 28
"Good luck!"

Insults and Negative Descriptions (figures 29–38)

Pão duro means literally "hard bread." The gesture (figure 29) is a fist and means a person is stingy, "He doesn't open his hand." A North American would say, "He's tightfisted." Figure 30, called either *burro* (donkey) or *tapado* (blinders), refers to the blinders put on horses or mules and indicates a person is narrow-minded. Figure 31, *barbeiro* (barber), or *navalha* (razor) is credited to São Paulo and means someone is a bad driver. The jaw is rubbed either with the knuckles or the upper half of the fingers, and the signer may use two fingers or all four. Of those who recognized this gesture, one offered the explanation that a bad barber will cut your face "just as a bad driver will cut your car." Another said the "barber" is used generally to suggest incompetence, though this gesture, reminiscent of the American expression "a close shave," seems to be reserved for bad drivers. Several women commented that they would shout *"Barbeiro!"* at a bad driver but would not use the gesture. A similar gesture recorded by Montgomery Merryman means someone is shameless. "The cheek is rubbed up and down with the backs of the fingers. (The gesture probably refers to blushing, one who does not or cannot blush being thus shameless. Generally the gesture is accompanied by the words, 'So and so hasn't this.')"[3] Figure 32 is similar to its American equivalent and means "He's crazy." The index finger can remain motionless or can tap or be rotated near the temple.

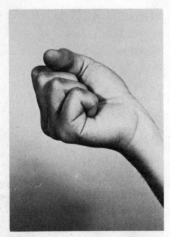

Figure 29
Pão duro, "He's stingy."

Figure 30
Burro or *tapado,* "Narrowminded!"

Figure 31
Barbeiro, "Bad driver!"

Figure 32
"You're crazy!"

Cornudo, literally "horned" (figure 33) is an insulting gesture directed toward a man whose wife is unfaithful. While this gesture might occur in joking behavior, it is generally insulting and so not used in view of the man so described lest it provoke a fight. A variant of this gesture provides the basis of a joke used primarily by children (figure 34). Either both index fingers or the first two fingers of one hand held to the back of the head imitate horns. Sometimes the expression *chifrudo* accompanies the gesture. Children (and a good number of adults) imitate such horns on unsuspecting persons being photographed. Two gestures indicate either a thief or a robbery. They can describe an occurrence, an object, or a person, but most likely the last, in which case they can be literal or symbolic, as one might describe a corrupt politician as a thief. In figure 35, the thumb of one hand is placed in the center of the open palm of the other hand. The gesture begins with the fingers of the first hand open and pointing upward. The hand and thumb are then twisted so that the gesture ends with the fingers pointing downward, and the movement can either be very quick or slow and dramatic. The second gesture (figure 36) is more imitative. One extends the hand at about waist level (the low position of the hand suggesting secrecy), fingers open, then quickly draws the hand back, closing the fingers, as

Figure 33
Cornudo

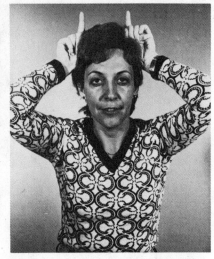

Figure 34
Cornudo

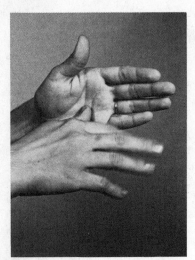

Figure 35
"Stolen," or "He's a thief."

Figure 36
"Stolen," or "He's a thief."

though snatching an object. A gesture indicating "jail" crosses the first two fingers of each hand to imitate the grating of bars on a jail window (figure 37). The phrase *Ver o sol nascer quadrado*, to see the sun squared (because it is seen through the barred windows), may accompany the gesture. This gesture may refer to a person who is in jail or to the probable consequence of an action. A gesture which can express anger, used sometimes with the expression "You won't see me even with binoculars" imitates looking through a spyglass. The same gesture might be used "when speaking of a loan, the payment of which is highly problematical. One might see his money with a spyglass but he would never get close enough to get it back"[4] (Fig. 38).

A gesture seen frequently in Brazil is the striking of a hard surface (or the signer's open palm on thigh; if a hard surface is not available) twice with the bottom of a clenched fist, generally accompanied by the phrase *Bem feito*, "well done." The expression is used sarcastically, and the combination of gesture and phrase can express a sense of smugness, arrogance, or genuine anger. No precise English equivalent exists, as the total effect combines "I told you so" and "It serves you right" with a disclaimer of responsibility. A gesture meaning to gossip or to speak badly of someone uses the first two fingers of either hand to imitate the snipping of a pair of scissors, derived "from the slang phrase *tesourar alguém*—to scissor someone."[5]

Figure 38
"You won't see me, even with binoculars!"

Figure 37
"You'll go to jail!"

Invitations to Eat or Drink (figures 39–42)

Several gestures indicate an invitation to drink. Figure 39 shows a gesture associated with alcohol. The arm is raised, thumb pointed toward mouth, the little finger extended. One might see the fingers closed or partially open. More common to men than to women, this gesture can serve as an invitation to have a drink or as a descriptive comment on having drunk a lot or on another person who drinks a lot. A very similar gesture is used in small bars and informal situations to ask for a drink. Thumb and little finger are extended, other fingers curled in against the palm, and the palm faces away from the signer. When used in this way, the hand is held away from the signer's face, with the thumb pointing up rather than at the mouth. Figure 40 refers to a small drink. Thumb and index finger are open at about one inch and the remaining fingers are closed against the palm. Called *traguinho*, little gulp or little swallow, it would probably not be used to indicate beer or wine, but might be used to indicate a small quantity of a strong liquor, an aperitif, or perhaps a cup of coffee, generally very strong and served in demitasse cups in Brazil. Figure 41, like 40 but with thumb and index finger closed, refers to coffee and mimics the holding of the demitasse cup. One might see the other hand held open, palm up, in imitation of the saucer. Less common than the gestures for drinking is one indicating "Let's eat" or "Come eat" (figure 42). The forearm is vertical, palm

Figure 39
Vamos tomar um trago, "Let's have a drink."

Figure 40
"Let's have coffee," or "Let's have a drink."

Figure 41
"Let's have coffee."

Figure 42
"Let's eat," or "Come eat."

open and held toward face, and the fingers are waved quickly, up and down in front of the mouth. The other hand may pat the stomach, but not necessarily. This gesture might also be used by older people to indicate something is easy, and might in that case be accompanied by the expression *É sopa* (It's a soup), *É canja* (It's chicken soup—like the American "duck soup") or *É café pequeno* (It's a little cup of coffee—like the American "small potatoes").[6]

More or Less (figures 43–45)

The single most frequently used gesture we observed means "I don't care," "More or less," "I don't know," "It's not important," and can be used in reference to just about anything and in just about any situation. The hands are held in front of the body, wrists loose, and the fingertips are brushed across each other, so the fingernails of one hand strike the fingertips of the other (figure 43). The brushing motion is then reversed and repeated, forward and back, several times. Another gesture with the same meaning but with somewhat ruder connotations is to brush the fingers under the chin (figure 44). While one common meaning of this gesture is "I don't know," it is used frequently with slightly different

Figure 43
"So, so." "More or less."
"I don't know."

Figure 44
"So, so." "More or less."
"I don't know."

Figure 45
Mais ou menos, "More or less."

connotation, perhaps suggesting disappointment or a sense of being left out or let down. The closest equivalent is the North American shrug of the shoulders. The phrase *"ficar na mão"* is used sometimes with the gesture but more often phrase and gesture are used separately. Literally, the phrase means "to stay in the hand," but the sense of the expression is to be left out, let down, disappointed. The palm is held toward the throat and the brushing motion, done with the fingertips, begins at the angle under the chin and moves forward, ending with the hand open and the palm up. *Mais ou menos* (figure 45), meaning "more or less," is another common gesture. It may use one hand or both, held open, palm down, fingers spread. The hand is rocked from side to side, the motion ranging from slow and deliberate to rapid, depending on the desired emphasis. It carries the suggestion of "I don't know," or "I don't care," but the more specific meaning is "So-so," "Not good, not bad."

No (figures 46 and 47)

Brazilians, like Americans, indicate "no" by shaking the head from side to side, but a common Brazilian hand gesture for "no" differs from American usage. The forearm is vertical, palm facing away from the body, index finger extended, other fingers closed. The extended finger, the hand, and perhaps the whole forearm are shaken *from side to side* (figure 46), and the gesture may be accompanied by the dental click (tsk, tsk) used by Americans to scold. The click (which may be used alone) and gesture mean simply "No" in Brazil, and though they may be used in an advisory way, they carry no connotations of scolding. As mentioned with children's gestures, Brazilians shake a finger at a child to scold, but in that case the finger is pointed and shaken at the child rather than from side to side. The difference between the two is important, as pointing at people is considered extremely rude, and shaking a finger at a person of equal status would probably be insulting. In Bahia, to be truly polite when counting people, one would *not* point at them with a finger because "you count animals that way." An emphatic "No!" might be indicated with both hands held at about chest level, wrists crossed, hands either open or closed except for index fingers (figure 47). The hands are pushed apart and away from the body. The gesture may be accompanied by a shake of the head, a dental click, or both. It may be used to

Figure 46   **Figure 47**
"No."   "No!"

mean something is finished or time is up. This gesture and the side-to-side shaking of the index finger might be accompanied by *"absolutamente!"* As John Tolman has pointed out, the word creates a problem for Americans, for whom it is strongly affirmative. It is strongly *negative* in Brazil.[7] As discussed earlier, when refusing an offer of food, "thanks" means "no." "No, thank you" is regarded as too blunt for a polite refusal.

Obscene Gestures (figure 48–52)

The following gestures are obscene, and though some might be used jokingly among friends or in informal situations, they are probably best avoided by the foreigner.

Brazilians tell countless jokes about North Americans who, intending to signify pleasure or approval (figure 48) by making a circle with thumb and index finger, are actually signaling "Screw you" in Brazilian gesture language (figure 49). The Brazilian gesture generally holds the hand low and the palm toward the body, and many Brazilians are aware of the North American gesture for "OK," but Americans in Brazil should avoid the gesture, substituting "thumbs up" (figure 27) to show approval or wish good luck. A discreet performance of this gesture might be done by holding the hand very close to the ear, resulting in a gesture similar to *daqui* (figure 57). Another highly obscene gesture, equivalent to "Up yours" in American slang, is slapping the top of a closed fist with the open palm of the other hand (figure 50). This gesture could be used to insult another person or to describe a bad situation, as an American might say, "I screwed the exam," but is extremely rude in either case. Though perhaps

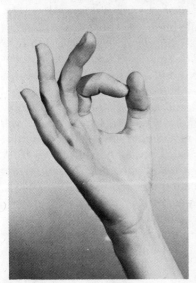

Figure 48
North American "O.K."

Figure 49
Brazilian "Screw you!"

Figure 50
"Screw you."
Extremely obscene.

unaware of their actions, Americans do use this gesture as an emphasizer and sometimes absentmindedly while thinking. A discreet variant of this gesture uses just one hand; the thumb is tapped lightly on a closed fist. Both are extremely rude. An obscene gesture used by men to threaten refers to the size of the male member. The hands are held in front of the body, palms toward one another and about one foot apart. One extremely obscene gesture, used rarely by men and never by women, involves jabbing the finger through a circle made with thumb and index finger of the opposite hand. Equally obscene is a gesture referring to masturbation. The hand is held in front of the body, palm cupped, and is shaken briskly from side to side.

Two gestures fall somewhat ambiguously into the obscene category. The gesture known generally as "the forearm jerk" or "the royal shaft" (figure 51) is called "banana" in Brazil, and while it can be obscene, it is not always as obscene in Brazil as it is elsewhere. It might be used as an insult, meaning "Screw you," but it might also be used to indicate that something is worthless or unimportant—"It's not worth a banana." We received conflicting reports from Brazilians, particularly from *paulistas*, which may indicate a passing fad, the limited informal use of an obscene gesture, or the existence of two slightly different gestures, such as

Figure 51
The *banana.* "It's not worth a banana." Also an obscene insult.

Figure 52
Saco cheio. "I'm fed up with it."

Laurence Wylie has documented in France. He describes this gesture performed with an open palm as "Va te faire foutre!, Go get yourself screwed! The word *foutre* is used so often and in so many different ways in French that it is even less strong than the English 'screw.'"[8] When the hand is closed in a fist, however, the gesture is "Le bras d'honneur!—The arm of honor: The Royal Shaft, the most *macho* of the gestures. A man's honor is shown to reside in the strength of his arm and fist, here vaunted as a phallic symbol."[9] Context, facial expression, and kinesics would doubtless establish the precise meaning of the Brazilian gesture, but given its questionable meaning, Americans are probably safest to avoid it. Some variations in performance include a single jerk of the forearm, without the slapping of the bicep, and, a more discreet version, a quick grasping of the forearm with the opposite hand. The second ambiguous gesture, used in a fairly casual manner to mean one is fed up with something, holds the hands in front of the body, anywhere from a few inches to a foot apart, thumb and index finger of each hand cupped with the other fingers folded against the palms (figure 52). The hands are shaken up and down. The phrase sometimes used with the gesture is "*Estou de saco cheio*," literally, "My bag is full." Although the reference is to fullness of the scrotum, women also use this gesture. Further, while all Brazilians recognize the anatomical reference, the gesture is not considered as obscene as the gestures in figures 48, 49 and 50. It is, however, considered inappropriate except in casual situations among friends and peers, and an American would probably do better to avoid the gesture than risk offending his audience.

Positive and Sympathetic Descriptions (figures 53–56)

Figure 53 shows a gesture used by both Brazilians and North Americans—tugging at one's lapels to indicate pride or importance. Figure 54 shows a similar Brazilian gesture, done by resting the thumbs near or under the armpits and wiggling the outstretched fingers of the hands. Glossed as *vida boa* (the good life), or *flauteando* (playing a flute), the gesture is used jokingly and means someone is lazy. The implication, however, is "He's got it made. He can afford to be lazy." *Dor de cotovelo*, literally, "elbow ache," indicates jealousy and is done by rubbing one elbow with the palm of the other hand (figure 55). It is generally used to

Figure 53
Indicates pride in self.

Figure 54
Vida boa, the good life.

Figure 55
Dor de cotovelo, "You're jealous."

Figure 56
Chupar o dedo, "You've been left out, disappointed."

describe another person and is generally reserved for romantic jealousy. Two explanations were offered for this gesture, one, that a person's elbows become sore when he is jealous because he rests his elbows on the table when he cries, and two, that jealousy is painful, like hitting one's elbow. *Chupar o dedo*, "to suck one's thumb," (figure 56) is used when someone is disappointed at being left out of something. It is used primarily in a teasing or coy manner rather than to describe a serious situation. It is more likely to be directed at someone else than to be used reflexively, and it is more likely to be heard as a proverbial expression than to be seen as a gesture.

Praise (figures 57–60)

A common gesture to indicate something is good is to pull the earlobe (figure 57). This gesture is used particularly with food, but could also describe other things—a person, an object, a dress. Often used with the expression *"É daqui, ó,"* literally, "from here," or *"jóia,"* "jewel," it means that the referent meets a certain standard. A stronger gesture of praise, meaning excellent or even sublime, is performed by kissing the tips of the fingers, then flicking the wrist forward and opening the fingers. It may be performed with a forward motion (figures 58 and 59) or a sideways motion (figure 60). Though less common than tugging the earlobe, these gestures can be used to praise anything. The semantic distinction between the two is slight, though some Brazilians interviewed associated the sideways motion with food and the forward motion with beauty. The gestures differ markedly, however, in performance. Both are dramatic. The first is much like a North American throwing a kiss. Most of the movement comes from the elbow, as the forearm is thrust forward. The second is a bit more complex. The hand, fingers vertical, is held slightly above and to one side of the lips. As the hand is pulled sideways, the fingertips are curled down and the signer kisses them as they pass the lips. The gesture ends at about cheekbone level on the opposite side of the face, being more compact than the former. A gesture used by men to praise a woman is the tracing of a silhouette with the hands. The shape of the silhouette is not, however, the hourglass figure praised by Americans, but rather a guitar-shaped figure, with a lower curve noticeably wider than the upper curve, as suits the Brazilian ideal of feminine shape.

Figure 57
Daqui! "Very good,
very nice."

Figure 58
"Excellent!"

Figure 59
"Excellent!"

Figure 60
"Excellent!"

Quantity and Size (figures 61–63)

A common gesture to indicate a place is full draws the fingers
and the thumb together, cupping the palm and sometimes
opening and closing the fingers (figure 61). One or both hands may
be used, and the gesture generally refers to people (bus drivers
use this gesture to indicate to waiting passengers that the bus is
full) but might be used with reference to objects. Striking one
index finger on the knuckle of the other index finger indicates

"half" (figure 62), as does striking one flat, open palm with the side of the other hand (figure 63).

Height and length are generally indicated as in North America, height by an open hand, palm down, and length or width by open hands, palms facing, held at an appropriate distance.

Figure 61
"Full." Refers particularly to people.

Figure 62
"Half."

Figure 63
"Half."

Time (figure 64)

Snapping the fingers can be used for emphasis or to get attention, but it can also have the specific meaning of "a long time ago." A gesture that indicates elapsed time uses the hand and arm (figure 64). The hand describes circles in the air while the arm moves away from the body. This gesture means "after." Merryman provides a slightly different meaning for the gesture when it is "accompanied by an affirmative nod of the head and a questioning expression. This gesture might mean, 'Does the agreement we made still hold?'; 'Will I see you later?'; 'Are you going there?', etc., referring to the last conversation or understanding."[10]

Figure 64
"After."

Notes

1. Laurence Wylie, *Beaux Gestes: A Guide to French Body Talk* (Cambridge, Mass.: The Undergraduate Press; New York: E.P. Dutton, 1977), p. viii.

2. Mark L. Knapp, *Nonverbal Communication in Human Interaction* (New York: Holt, Rinehart & Winston, Inc., 1972), p. v.

3. Montgomery Merryman, *Portuguese—A Portrait of the Language of Brazil* (Rio: Pongetti, 1945; São Paulo: União Cultural Brazil-Estados Unidos, 1951), p. 157.

4. Merryman, *Portuguese*, p. 159.

5. Merryman, *Portuguese*, p. 158.

6. American equivalents suggested by Alfred Hower, University of Florida, personal communication, November 3, 1981.

7. Jon Tolman, University of New Mexico, personal communication, November 17, 1981.

8. Wylie, *Beaux Gestes*, p. 72.

9. Wylie, *Beaux Gestes*, p. 77.

10. Merryman, *Portuguese*, p. 159.

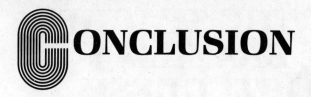# CONCLUSION

The preceding materials do not pretend to encompass every detail of Brazilian nonverbal communication. As described in the Introduction, Brazil is a large country with many distinctive regions and a number of socioeconomic classes. No observer, especially a foreign observer, is likely to catch all the possible variations in custom and behavior. Our methodology precluded our gathering of certain kinds of data, and finally, our interest here is in human behavior which is subject to constant change. Specific gestures may come and go according to current trends. Shifting values and social structure will result in alterations to and adaptations of nonverbal expression. Neither verbal nor nonverbal communication systems are static; hence the reader must be prepared to update his knowledge through his own experiences in Brazil.

The fact that language changes hardly nullifies the utility of dictionaries. Likewise, the fact that nonverbal systems change does not nullify the utility of a general description like our own. Our intention is not to make Brazilians of North Americans, but rather to provide guidelines, descriptions, and explanations to prepare Americans for interaction within a different system with different rules and different values. *Boa sorte!*

TO THE TEACHER of BRAZILIAN PORTUGUESE

The preceding pages provide a body of information on Brazilian behavior, culture, and language that concerns both specific and general situations and attitudes. The first difficulty facing the language teacher interested in nonverbal communication is the incorporation of such material into a doubtless already overflowing syllabus, and few published materials exist to provide specific strategies for the teaching of nonverbal communication. Within the existing materials, the teaching of gestures has probably received more attention than the teaching of nonverbal communication as we have used the term. Fernando Poyatos, *Man Beyond Words: Theory and Methodology of Nonverbal Communication* (New York: State English Council, 1976) provides a detailed and comprehensive study of the kinds, meanings, and uses of nonverbal communication and includes suggestions for fieldwork projects as well as projects using narrative literature. Mark L. Knapp's *Nonverbal Communication in Human Interaction* (New York: Holt, Rinehart & Winston, 1972) and the accompanying instructor's manual bring together a highly readable general survey of nonverbal communication and specific exercises for use in the classroom. Knapp's *Essentials of Nonverbal Communication* (New York: Holt, Rinehart & Winston, 1980) contains further information highly useful to students and teachers. Sahnny Johnson's *A Handbook on Nonverbal Communication for Teachers of Foreign Languages* (forthcoming), designed expressly for the foreign language teacher who may be new to the study of nonverbal communication, provides both general methodology and specific strategies for the inclusion of nonverbal communication in the language classroom. Sandra Bunker's *An Illustrated Gestural Inventory: Latin-American Gestures for English-Speaking Students of Spanish* (MA Thesis, Brigham Young Univ., 1978), includes a number of specific strategies for the teaching of gesture, as do Robert Saitz, "Gestures in the Language Classroom," *English Language Teaching* 27 (1966): 33–37, and Jerald R. Green, *A Gesture Inventory for the Teaching of Spanish* (New York: Chilton Books, 1968). The following suggestions and observations stem from workshops conducted at Indiana University, Bloomington, Indiana in November, 1981, and at the University of North Carolina, Chapel Hill, North Carolina in January, 1982, where we were able to test in classroom situations both our materials and some of the strategies suggested in the above named studies.

Sahnny Johnson summarizes the processes involved in the teaching/learning of language behavior.

As in the learning of the foreign language itself, the discovery procedure moves through several stages:

    1) the student's realization that his own native-language behavior is systematic or rule-governed;

    2) the further realization that his system is not the only possible system, or the most logical, or the most advanced, but just one of many systems—the result of a long series of arbitrary choices;

    3) the study of the particulars of another system;

    4) the actual production of another system.[1]

In the first two stages, the instructor might use examples, first of native and then of foreign patterns, which could be drawn from magazines, photographs, film, or even literature. Directed observation will also help students to raise their awareness of nonverbal communication, and an instructor might ask students to observe particular situations (formal restaurants, student cafeterias, grocery stores, churches, etc.) and particular patterns of behavior (eye contact, use of hands or feet, postures). When comparing their observations in class, students can begin to analyze the meaning of particular patterns and to distinguish general from individual behavior patterns. Students might also be asked to break some of the rules they observe, paying careful attention to the responses their behavior brings. In the second and third stages, the instructor might invite native speakers of the target language into the classroom, or might suggest that students direct their out-of-class observation toward foreign students or foreign communities, again providing specific suggestions of situations and behavior patterns for observation and analysis.

The teaching of specific gestures is probably the easiest way to introduce stages three and four. Students on any level find gesture interesting and fun, and most students can become fairly proficient at using specific gestures which do not exist in the students' native language (such as *dor do cortovelo* or *barbeiro)* or with gestures which have different meanings in the different cultures (the American "OK" or the Brazilian *figa)*. Either type of gesture illustrates the fact that gestures, like language, are culture specific. The inclusion of a gesture or gestures could be a standard addition to each week's lessons or vocabulary, particularly since specific gestures are often directly relevant to words, situations, or concepts covered in class. Gestures can frequently be incorporated into existing dialogs, or Bunker suggests asking students to write their own dialogs around a list of specific gestures. The instructor should be sure to provide contextual information when introducing a gesture—when or where the gesture might be used, or between what groups of people—and might invent a typical situation to illustrate a given gesture. Gestures, like words, have both connotative and denotative meanings, and language students must cultivate both.

The teacher's task becomes more difficult when one moves from specific gestures to broader concerns, like eye and body contact, in part because matters like gaze and personal space are learned almost unconsciously and are accepted as a part of "natural" interactional behavior. Such matters lack the dramatic-performance quality of gestures. As sustained patterns of behavior, they prove to be more difficult for foreigners to accept and to master, while their pervasiveness makes them a constant influence on any and all interactions. Nonverbal greetings serve as a good bridge from specific gestures to these broader concerns, including the gestural handshake, *abraço,* or kiss, and the proxemic/kinesic elements of distance, duration, and eye contact. The instructor must be prepared to demonstrate, watch, and correct, pointing out switches from Brazilian to American behavior patterns, and might want to use devices like stop watches and measuring tapes to mark differences clearly. For example, American students were asked to shake hands warmly with another student of the same sex. In most cases, the handshakes were accomplished with nearly outstretched arms, lasted for two or three "pumps," and included steady eye contact. Then, each student was asked to repeat the handshake, taking one step closer to his partner. Invariably, as the distance was shortened, eye contact was broken, and students at either distance had difficulty maintaining the handshake for any length of time. Such automatic responses provide excellent grounds for discussing the communicative impact of nonverbal communication, and greeting exercises can be used independently or as a standard part of dialog and conversation practice.

The most difficult patterns for most American students are probably the incorporation of increased eye and body contact and decreased personal distance during casual conversation. While these patterns can easily be explained and demonstrated on any level, extensive practice might best be left to more advanced classes, and even advanced students find sustained simultaneous concentration on foreign verbal and nonverbal systems difficult. Thus, the instructor might want to use previously memorized dialogs and careful "stage directions" when teaching these conversational patterns. The playing of specific roles provides both practice and material for discussion, particularly when students are assigned conflicting roles regarding the use of eye/body contact, gesture, or personal proxemics. The instructor might also emphasize such patterns through example rather than actual practice, bringing in photographs from target language magazines or (when possible) inviting native speakers into the classroom. Students should be encouraged to discuss their responses to foreign patterns, whether their exposure to that pattern stems from experience or observation, from real situations or created examples.

Regardless of the specific methods and precise amount of time an instructor chooses to devote to the teaching of nonverbal communication, two basic principles should be emphasized. First, verbal and nonverbal systems function together, repeating, substituting, contradicting, and accenting, so cross cultural fluency demands knowledge and practice of both.[2] Second, these two systems are part of a still larger cultural worldview; differing speech and behavior patterns may well reflect deeper cultural differences in attitudes and values, logical and consistent to the initiated, but baffling to the outsider.

Notes

1. *A Handbook on Nonverbal Communication for Teachers of Foreign Languages* (forthcoming, Newbury House), p. 144

2 *Ibid.*, cf. Chapter 12, "Pedagogical Suggestions," pp. 151–80.